Praise for

OWN THE CLOUDS

"BREAKTHROUGH the clouds! Discover the power within yourself to venture into the future by using the simple principles found in Own the Clouds."

—BRIAN BIRO
BEST-SELLING AUTHOR, AMERICA'S BREAKTHROUGH COACH

"As a Wall Street professional for nearly two decades, I can easily say that in this book you'll get rarely shared insights on what actually goes on behind closed doors, which can make a difference in your decisions."

—ROWLAND WILHELM
VICE PRESIDENT DIRECTOR OF SALES REAVES ASSET MANAGEMENT

"Own the Clouds helps you analyze cloud companies. It breaks down this complicated world and puts it into practical terms a layperson can understand. If you want to ride the next wave of technological growth, read this book!"

—ALLEN FAHDEN
AUTHOR, INNOVATION SPEAKER, TRAINER TO FORTUNE 500
COMPANIES, AND CREATOR OF THE ONE-MILLION-COPY
BEST-SELLING TEAM DIMENSIONS PROFILE

"Own the Clouds helps you appreciate the promise of cloud computing and the opportunities that lie ahead."

—GARRETT SUTTON
ESQ., SUTTON LAW CENTER, BEST-SELLING AUTHOR,
SPEAKER, AND RICH DAD ADVISOR

"As an insurance professional and amateur racer, after reading this book I realized that cloud computing companies are like off-road motorcycle racing, which I love to do. It's constantly changing and fast paced. You had better know what you are doing at all times, and have a great pit crew. Own the Clouds is your pit crew that keeps you on track and pointed in the right direction so you can enjoy the ride!"

—BRYAN LEMOINE
VITA SECURUS INSURANCE SERVICES

"You'll get the benefit of decades of hands-on experience explained and laid out in a concise manner. I believe this book, Own the Clouds is a must-read for everyone attempting to understand the inner workings of this coming wave of technology."

—JOSEPH E. MEYER
PRESIDENT OF MEYER AND ASSOCIATES,
EDITOR OF STRAIGHTMONEYANALYSIS.COM

"Own the Clouds gives us a peek into the future of technology in a way most of us don't have time to uncover on our own, and probably wouldn't understand even if we stumbled across it. An important read if technology is a word you use regularly!"

—LARRY MANDELBERG
SACRAMENTO BUSINESS JOURNAL

"Optimal health is wealth you can't buy. Financial success is freedom to organize your life around what matters most. Own the Clouds is an important book to understanding key elements of cloud computing."

—DR. WAYNE SCOTT ANDERSEN
BEST-SELLING AUTHOR OF DR. A'S HABITS OF HEALTH,
CO-FOUNDER AND MEDICAL DIRECTOR OF TAKE SHAPE FOR LIFE ®,
CO-FOUNDER AND CHAIRMAN OF THE HEALTH INSTITUTE

"When I picked up this book, I knew nothing about The Four Key Cloud Elements and just enough about technology to get in trouble. I honestly thought this was going to put me to sleep. I was wrong. I LOVED IT! This book grabbed me from the first paragraph. I even read parts to total strangers. You must get a copy and read this book. It will totally change how you think."

—AMANDA DECKER
CERTIFIED NUTRITION AND OPTIMAL HEALTH SPECIALIST,
GLOBAL DIRECTOR OF TAKE SHAPE FOR LIFE ®

"A star is born! When it comes to shedding light on technology and investing, Own the Clouds is your destiny."

—PEGGY MCCOLL
NEW YORK TIMES BEST-SELLING AUTHOR

"Own the Clouds *is better than a terabyte! This book explains why it's important for readers to embrace cloud technology, and then it goes one step further and actually shows you how to drill down and expose cloud computing companies using free internet software.*"

—VIET THAI
NCS COMPUTERS

"Own the Clouds *is a very interesting book and makes a great case for everyone to take a look at this very seriously. The book is written in a language simple enough for most people to understand, and still the technical details are covered in great detail. A must-read for any person who believes in the future of technology.*"

—RAJ KARTHIKEYAN
CEO AND FOUNDER OF SACRAMENTO EDUCATIONAL WORKSHOPS

"Own the Clouds *is a riveting read that will expand your view on the next shift that's coming: cloud computing. When you're finished reading this book, you'll quickly understand the leverage, speed, and agility a cloud-based company has, and the opportunities in this rapidly growing space.*"

—TODD LAY
TODD LAY INTERNATIONAL, AND FOUNDER OF
SIMPLEBACKOFFICE.COM

"*A must-read for consumers,* Own the Clouds *is one of the most important books I've seen on cloud computing—the new 'utility' era that is already affecting the way people across the globe live, work, and communicate. This book is the ultimate guide to learning what clouds are, how they affect you, and how to find them.*"

—IVAN MISNER
NEW YORK TIMES BEST-SELLING AUTHOR,
FOUNDER OF BNI ® AND REFERRAL INSTITUTE ®

"*I've got notes in the margins. I'm hooked. This book is awesome! My fiancé had to pry it out of my hands to get a peek! He's going to have to get his own copy of* Own the Clouds *because he can't have mine.*"

—KATIE SIMMONS
MORTGAGE PLANNER

"Awesome book! Growing up in the era when TV's had rabbit ears, I realize more than ever that technology is here to stay and evolving. This book has given me a way to move into the future. At last, I feel less like a greenhorn and more like a pro. Thank you, Own the Clouds."

—LYNNE P. THOMSON
THE PROUTY RANCH HISTORIC SITE ON THE
PONY EXPRESS ROUTE, PLACERVILLE, CA

"All along I've been telling people that computers are a fad. Admittedly, that was to prove my ignorance of technology. Maybe the clouds will prove me right after all. It will be fun to dust off this book 10-20 years from now and compare!"

—LONNIE J. RUSH
MANAGING PARTNER OF RCM PARTNERS FUND

"Own the Clouds is an insightful look at the influence cloud computing is having on our everyday personal and business lives. There are many major companies in this arena that come to mind when thinking about cloud computing, but most importantly, those flying under the radar who are growing exponentially. This book provides sound advice that novices and experts alike can clearly grasp as well as great tips for finding the next winners in the cloud space!"

—JOHN RIZZO
MANAGING PARTNER OF GLOBEONDEMAND

"My kids, and especially my boys, are totally wrapped up in technology and cloud applications (apps). They know way more than me about all this stuff, but as soon as I started reading Own the Clouds, something clicked. I admit I won't turn into an overnight cloud wiz kid, but this book has broadened how I look at the entire area, and I'm confident in time it will have a positive impact on my life."

—GLEN SEWELL
INDEPENDENT INSURANCE AGENT AND FATHER OF FOUR

"I was pleasantly surprised by Own the Clouds. Unlike most books on what's considered a dry subject, this is sprinkled with humor and more than once made me laugh. On a serious note, I found The Four Key Cloud Elements powerful tools that I will definitely use."

—PAUL CANALE M.D.
CANALE SPINE INSTITUTE

"This first-of-its-kind book is going to make a difference in your life, and the lives of others. When you purchase a copy of Own the Clouds, *a portion of the author's proceeds is donated to support sick and hungry kids through a variety of charities, starting with the Kiwanis Family House, the Ronald McDonald House, Shriner's Hospitals for Children, and food banks. I'd call this a win-win for everyone!"*

—MAX WOODFORD
PRESIDENT OF LIFE CONNECT ADVANTAGE,
KIWANIS CLUB OF CITRUS HEIGHTS

*"*Own the Clouds *provides a step-by-step roadmap for finding technology companies that even non-technical folks can follow…a valuable guide for us all."*

—RITA BEALL
SVP CENTRAL OPERATIONS MANAGER FOR RIVER CITY BANK,
BOARD OF DIRECTOR FOR THE KIWANIS FAMILY HOUSE, AND VICE
PRESIDENT OF THE GREATER SACRAMENTO KIWANIS CLUB

*"*Own the Clouds *is the voice of reason I'd been waiting for to move forward with confidence and a plan."*

—JOHN USSERY
SENIOR ACCOUNT EXECUTIVE FOR TELEPACIFIC COMMUNICATIONS

*"*Own the Clouds *is heavenly! This book simplifies and demystifies the complex nature of bulls, bears, and clouds. My fears have decreased and my confidence has increased. Now I can speak intelligently with my family and friends. I'm walking on clouds!"*

—SUE PEPPERS
AUTHOR OF RECESSION BLESSINGS AND SONIC BOOMERS,
PRESIDENT OF PEPPERS TV, INC.

"We were toddlers back in 1986 when Microsoft first went public. Who knew it would grow up to be a giant in the world of technology. Today, our child is a toddler. Wouldn't it be great to find the next tech superstar for her when she's our age? Own the Clouds definitely got us thinking and looking for that next big super-cloud."

—LANA AND VITALY (LEE) BATISHEV
GLOBAL DIRECTORS OF TAKE SHAPE FOR LIFE *

"I'm the person who stands in line to be the first to own the newest iPad. I love technology and use it every day. As I was reading Own the Clouds, my first thought was this book would be helpful for my parents to read—and then it hit me. This book made me curious to find out how to get started, and to figure out which cloud companies will fill the next important technology niche! Knowledge is what you'll get from this book, and with knowledge you'll have confidence to act."

—STEPHANIE GOLKA
GLOBAL DIRECTOR OF TAKE SHAPE FOR LIFE®

"As a business owner and IT professional, I essentially use the cloud every day without really thinking about it. Insightful and forward-thinking, Own the Clouds is the perfect book, and at the right time for those who want to get ahead and learn more about how this all fits together."

—JERAMIE WHEELER
PRESIDENT AND CEO OF AIRTOP TECHNOLOGY GROUP, INC.

"Explore your possibilities. Explore the clouds so you can own them…on purpose!"

—KEVIN W. MCCARTHY
AUTHOR OF THE ON-PURPOSE PERSON AND
THE ON-PURPOSE BUSINESS

"Go BIG. Go CLOUDS!"

—BRIAN SHARP
GO BIG COMPANY

OWN
THE
CLOUDS

The First Guide to Investing in
Cloud Computing Companies

Joyce Blonskij

AUTHORITY
PUBLISHING

Own the Clouds: The First Guide to Investing in Cloud Computing Companies
By Joyce Blonskij
1. Business & Economics : E-Commerce - General 2. Business & Economics : Investments & Securities - Stocks 3. Business & Economics : Personal Finance - Investing
ISBN: 978-1-935953-21-0

Cover design by Lewis Agrell

Printed in the United States of America

Authority Publishing
11230 Gold Express Dr. #310-413
Gold River, CA 95670
800-877-1097
www.AuthorityPublishing.com

Own the Clouds is dedicated to: My clients.

My best friend and husband, John Blonskij.

In loving memory of my parents, Max and Rosina.

To everyone who has ever dreamed.

To visionaries who make dreams come true!

CONTENTS

Part I: Understanding Clouds

1. Discovering Clouds 1
2. Make Way for Clouds 13
3. Cloud Realities 21

Part II: A Pathway into Clouds

4. Global Clouds Connect 33
5. Clouds on the Ground 45
6. Sifting through Clouds 53

Part III: The Four Key Cloud Elements

7. Polar Clouds - Sky-High 67
8. Cirrus Clouds - Lifting the Veil 85
9. Stratus Clouds - Out in the Open 97
10. Cumulus Clouds - Charting the Clouds.......................... 107

Part IV: The Process

11. Cloud Control 133
12. Tracking Clouds - Blueprint 145

About the Author...153

Acknowledgments...157

Giving Back 159

Exhibit No.1: Summary Page - Yahoo Finance...............160

Notes 161

Resources..169

Index...177

PART I:

UNDERSTANDING CLOUDS

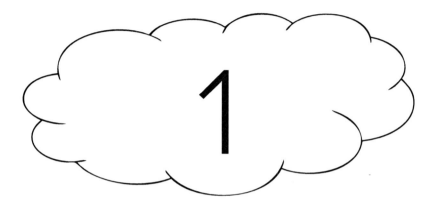

DISCOVERING
CLOUDS

"I only hope that we don't lose sight of one thing – that it was all started by a mouse."

WALT DISNEY

You are standing on the brink of the next utility era and it's called **cloud computing**.

Looking back in history, the first Westbound trip to deliver the mail took 9 days and 23 hours.[1] It was overpriced at $5 a half-ounce.[2] Mail carriers rode hard for 2,000 miles, starting in St. Joseph, Missouri, and passing through my hometown of Sacramento, California, until reaching their final destination of San Francisco. It was fast and the most direct way to deliver the mail. I'm talking about the Pony Express and their famous horses and riders. Once Pacific Telegraph completed their lines, the Pony Express was put out of business after only 19 months.

When you think of mail today, you can send a letter across the country in three to four days, or, you can e-mail, which is almost instantaneous.

New technology keeps evolving. It's how we connect and come together. Pull out your cell phone in San Francisco, and make a call to New York City, using 4G technology – you're connected in less than 60 seconds!

Take a look at Facebook. In October 2010, 200 million people around the world were actively using Facebook from a phone, which more than tripled in just one year.[3] Six months later, April 2011, Facebook added another fifty million mobile users.[4] More than 600 million people around the world are logging in from cell phones, laptops, or PCs to chat with family and friends – and this number is climbing.[5]

Every person using e-mail, cell phones and Facebook have at least one thing in common: they are all cloud computing.

What Are Cloud Computing Companies?

Cloud computing companies are businesses focused on the Internet and the world of wireless devices. They provide resources like software, hardware, security, analysis, and data on demand. These companies advance the Internet and wireless technology every time they introduce a new application or develop a new technology. Cloud companies are bringing you new-and-improved cutting-edge devices and discoveries that change everything. They affect how you live, work, and play.

There is no doubt in my mind that social networks and e-business applications are here to stay. As an investor, you need to be constantly looking for those cloud-based companies that are making a difference.

I am often asked how I sift through all the information to find cloud companies in which to invest. By the time you're finished reading this book, you'll have a good foundation to make many of these decisions on your own, whether you're a beginner or an experienced investor. If you're looking to invest a portion of your money in cloud computing companies, this book is for you.

Basic Clouds

This book started out as a report for my clients to explain and to help educate them on cloud computing. They needed some background and frankly, it's important for us to share common ground when deciding what companies to consider owning. In the course of my work, I realized that millions of people have listened to an ad or read something about "clouds" and "cloud computing," but may still be unsure of what it all means. They may have a basic idea of clouds, but if you were to ask them to explain what a cloud is, they would have a tough time.

Own the Clouds will quickly get you up to speed on what the heck this cloud computing and cloud company stuff is all about. You'll take a look back to see how this all came to be, and a look forward to where cloud computing is taking you.

This book will be your how-to guide and manual that gently guides and teaches you how to find cloud opportunities. After reading a few chapters, you may decide that never in a million years would you want to tackle this by yourself, and that's okay. *Own the Clouds* will give you a leg up when you talk with your kids, or when you're on the golf course or with your financial advisor. They'll be impressed by how much you know.

Fad or Fact

Think cloud computing is a passing fad? You're not seeing the big picture. In 1943 the chairman of IBM, Thomas Watson, went on record with this statement:

"I think there is a world market for maybe five computers." [6]

I bet he wishes he could take that statement back. He didn't see the future of computers very clearly. It's impossible to be exact on the number of computer users in the world today, but there are several companies who attempt to measure the Internet's usage: Nielsen Ratings, Mediametrix, Serverwatch, and the Computer Industry Almanac (CIA). These and other groups use custom techniques of polling, electronic tallying of server traffic, web server logging, focus group sampling, and other measurement means. They estimate that more than 223 million Americans used the Internet in 2010! [7]

Fad

In 1879 Thomas Edison, one of our most prolific inventors, and the person who patented the first electric light bulb, said: "The radio craze will die out in time."[8] Edison was right. The radio craze did die out. But it took more than 125 years for his prediction to come true.

In 1949, Popular Mechanics Magazine put their reputation on the line by forecasting: "Computers in the future may weigh no more than 1.5 tons."[9] They miscalculated that one to say the least. But heck ... who's counting?

Fact

- It took 38 years for radio to reach 50 million users.

- It took 13 years for TV to reach 50 million users.

- It took 4 years for the Internet to reach 50 million users.

- It only took 3 years for the iPod to reach 50 million users.[10]

March 11, 2011, Japan was hit by a powerful 8.9 magnitude earthquake followed by a severe tsunami that knocked out the country's phone system. One hour after the quake hit, 1,200 tweets per minute began posting from Tokyo.[11] At the end of the month, Twitter reported handling 1 billion world-wide tweets per week.[12]

New discoveries in technology are changing how you communicate with family and friends and do business. Every day you are becoming more and more connected through computers, cell phones, and the Internet. Ways of doing things are changing. Devices are going above and beyond what you used to take for granted. Technology is creating a new way of life and a new language. The Internet is creating businesses. From reading the news to posting your vacation photos online, the Internet is how you receive and send information. The possibilities are endless, thanks in part to those innovative developers and code crackers who work day and night writing programs for all our wireless gadgets.

Look at how you get information. It finds you through the Internet and your mobile phone and wireless devices. Eighteen of the 25 largest newspapers are experiencing record declines in circulation.[13] Why? The Internet is taking over. You don't have to walk down the driveway to get the news. You don't have to drive to the grocery store parking lot with a bunch of quarters to open a paper rack. Push a power-on button and you have news. The Kindle e-book reader outsold paper books in 2010's Christmas season. Why? It's easy, convenient, and comes to us by way of the Internet.

Today, computers and cameras are practically microscopic. They are fast and affordable. Kids carry them around like chewing gum in their back pockets — they don't leave home without them!

Tech Tune-Up

1. Do you believe the Internet is here to stay?

2. Do you see the use of electronic devices becoming such a part of your life that you just can't do without them?

3. Do you see the younger generation embracing the Internet and mobile devices?

4. Do you, your family, co-workers, neighbors, and friends get some or all of your news off the Internet or your cell phone?

5. Have you ever bought airline or movie tickets from the Internet?

6. Have you ever watched a video or posted a photo on the Internet?

7. Do you use e-mail?

8. Do you pay your bills online or know someone who does?

9. Have you ordered photos or medication online?

10. Have you bought books or music from an Internet site?

If you answered yes … Congratulations! You've been cloud computing on some level.

Cloud Buzz

For those of you still scratching your head over what clouds are and how they may or may not be different from the Internet, let me say this: **cloud computing is a fancy way of saying "the Internet" and all things wireless**. It's the new buzzword.

When you work off of a software program that's installed on your personal computer, you are not in the clouds. As soon as you connect to the Internet or use a wireless device, you are in the clouds.

On March 29, 2011, Cloudtweaks.com wrote: "'the cloud' is not another industry buzzword, but a broad category which will drive the next phase of IT projects. For IT and business managers already inundated with information about the promise of a cloud centric infrastructure the question is not whether or not to use the cloud, but how. [sic]" [14]

When you transmit information remotely — using an Internet device like a cell phone or iPad, reading news from a website, or sending an e-mail — you are cloud computing. When you put it all together, "the cloud" is not just another tech-created buzzword, but a new, dynamic way to communicate, get information, and do business that is going to drive the next phase of Internet growth. It's the new land-grab race in which companies are scooping up market share with the expectation that more and more consumers and business partners get involved "in the clouds."

In time you'll hear different terms and variations of cloud-supported companies, such as "cloud dust." These would be those little companies that spring up and add services and value. "Blue clouds" could refer to recycle services, while "green clouds" promote and support our environment. At the end of the day, they all refer to a network of wireless virtual sources for navigating the web.

Intermediate Clouds

There are those of you tech-minded investors out there who know exactly what cloud computing is all about, and are interested in learning how to find and invest in cloud companies but need some help getting started. I realized just how important it is to share this information…and here you are.

Own the Clouds is not a book on timing the market or how to pick penny stocks. You won't get a copy of my stock list. You will learn how it's done. Once you know how to find clouds, you can invest for a lifetime. You may have heard the saying, "Give a man a fish and he can eat for a day, but teach a man how to fish and he can eat for a lifetime." You are going fishing and I will be your guide! Teaching you the skills you need instead of giving you a one-time list of stocks in this book was an easy decision. It is what's best for you. By the time you read this book, that list could have, and most likely will have, changed to some degree. You need to know how to find clouds. After going through the steps I've outlined, you'll know how to find cloud companies, what to look for, and questions you need answered. At some point you may want to turn this over to a professional but first things first: you need to start by learning some of the basic concepts. By the time you reach the end of this book you will have the ability to recognize, analyze and discuss cloud computing.

Skills and Tools

I'm going to share a number of skills and tools I use to uncover clouds.

- ✓ You'll learn techniques to identify visionary cloud companies that develop, produce, service, and evolve using science and technology.
- ✓ You'll learn to determine whether a cloud company is growing, viable, and profitable, which is important to know as a stockholder.
- ✓ You'll learn the Four Key Cloud Elements needed for investing in cloud computing companies, and how to use them when making investment decisions.
- ✓ You'll learn how to stay current and on top of old and new clouds as they roll in.
- ✓ You'll get resources and links that will help you on your journey.

The Future of Clouds

In Chapter 3, there is a link to a short video called, "A Day Made of Glass." I'd love for you to take a moment and watch this. You'll get a good idea of what you are going to be doing in the near future. Much of what you will see in this video is already in the pipeline and is truly amazing. Go to YouTube and check out this video right now.

Cyber Safety

If you have ever broke your cell phone, or have kids who want to play on your iPad, in Chapter 4 I will be sharing with you "7 Ways to Keep Your Devices Safe."

Business owners and managers, concerned about privacy issues surrounding company data, there is a section at the end of Chapter 4 with pertinent information about storing critical data in the clouds.

Advanced Clouds

Experienced investors who understand and embrace cloud computing and are looking for ways to invest, *Own the Clouds* is especially for you!

Since you already know most of the basics about cloud computing, you can move quickly through the first couple of chapters.

In Chapter 6, you'll get a list of questions to ask when considering a cloud computing company. I want you to have them now, so you can start thinking and formulating ideas about clouds.

Cloud Q + A:

1. Is there a market for the company's products or services?

2. Is there a need for their products or services?

3. Is there a desire for their products or services?

4. Can the company deliver the goods and/or services as promised?

5. What's their track record?

6. Can the company provide value as good as or better than their competitors?

7. Would you buy the company's products or use their services?

8. Would you recommend the company to others and be a repeat customer?

9. Can you see, down the road, the company adding services, clients, or customers and posting profits?

If your answers are YES! then it's time to go to work. With thousands of publicly traded companies and more on the way, you have a lot to look at and mull over, which is a very good reason to get started as soon as possible.

The Four Key Cloud Elements

The Four Key Cloud Elements to investing in cloud computing companies are laid out for you in Part III. **This is the heart of the book.** You will want to use these chapters as a resource in the future.

Here are three points related to cloud computing companies I want you to start thinking about now:

- Who are the top providers?

- Who manufactures their products?

- Is there a low-cost provider that's crushing competition?

Consider all the possibilities and then ask, What have I missed?

The Process

In Part IV you'll learn how to apply a process to keep current and fresh. You'll get a daily and weekly blueprint to quickly check off items as you go down your to-do list. And – in this section, you'll find my two best tips for investing.

Exclusive Offer

For the do-it-yourself folks who would like a little help, I am offering you direct access to me. This exclusive one-time offer is available to those who purchase *Own the Clouds*. It's on the house! I am happy to answer a quick question that gets you through all the noise Wall Street makes. **Your exclusive OFFER CODE is found in the "*About the Author*" section of this book.**

Whether you're investing on your own or with the help of a financial professional, you always need to diversify your holdings, understand the risks, and not put all your eggs in one basket. That said, there is still no assurance that you'll make money or protect against a loss in the event of an overall market drop or unexpected bad news.

Every investor is unique, and the amount and percentage of funds allocated to clouds will vary depending on your needs. I strongly recommend that before you begin any investing you get some help from a professional investment advisor. It may save you time and money down the road. Keep in mind, whether you're a beginner or an experienced investor, to *follow the money* and when possible, get ahead of the trend — they go hand in hand.

Look for visionary cloud companies and business leaders that are going to make their mark on generations yet to be born. Back in the early 1950s, Walt Disney had a vision for a theme park for children. His hard work and imagination has become the benchmark and standard in family entertainment. It started with an inspiration and a cartoon character called Mickey the mouse. Today Disney is global! With theme parks, movies, and family-focused vacations, "Disney" is a buzzword that's recognized from one end of the planet to the other. **Disney has gone viral**! You'll see that I start each chapter with one of his quotes. They highlight his talent, vision, hard work and passion. From the entertainment industry to cloud computing, visionaries can and will make a difference in the lives of generations to come.

I want you to have a good experience and do well. So put on your thinking cap, grab a pen, dig out a highlighter and get ready to put your head in the clouds. Before you know it, you'll be a cloud-tech-detective and on your way to finding those silver-lined clouds. As Bill Gates, founder of Microsoft, said, "The next sea change is upon us."[15]

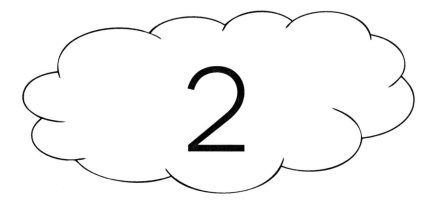

MAKE WAY FOR CLOUDS

"The era we are living in today is a dream come true."

WALT DISNEY

Growing up in the '60s, I remember our old-fashioned black-and-white TV set. Furniture with rabbit ears! I had to move the antenna around in order to pick up a good signal, which would bring in the station we wanted to watch. Fast-forward to the early 1970s. My first computer experience was in junior college, coming face to face with something called an IBM key-punch machine. It was a huge thing you sat at and punched keys and buttons. These were the same machines our government used to punch out and print green Social Security checks.

In 1985 when I started my financial services career, the Wall Street firm where I worked was using state-of-the-art DOS-based computers. I shared a monster computer with another financial advisor. It was parked between our desks on a turnstile. This bad boy was big, bulky and hard to use. As time passed, our monitors got some color. They called it "amber." Clients would "ooh" and "aah" while we watched stock trades flash on the screen in black and amber lights. It was impressive, but by today's standards, it's prehistoric.

Today, I can acquire stock quotes and initiate trades from anywhere on the planet as long as I have a device and an Internet connection!

Before the Internet or cell phones were developed, if you were out and needed to make a phone call, you looked for a corner phone booth. When you spotted the red-painted booth, you hoped no one had walked off with the phone book, the phone worked, and that you had enough change with you to make the call. I am talking ancient history compared to what we have today.

Remember how happy you were when you got your first bag phone — those clunky black leather bags that weighed at least seven pounds? You proudly carried it everywhere you went. You were a big shot then.

Bag phones stepped aside to be replaced by a solid piece of plastic that broke as easily as your crystal wine glass. These little gems were pushed off the store shelves by devices called "flips" and "sliders." Then, smartphones arrived and you could browse the Internet, take photos and post comments on social sites. The problem with these smartphones is texting. You type on tiny little keyboard buttons, or on a smooth surface that has a mind of its own when it comes to spelling. Forget it if you are clumsy, have bad eyes or big fingers.

Today, my tech buddies carry wireless devices in very professional black leather cases. The new devices are as thin as a pancake and as tough as steel. They can surf the web, schedule appointments, shop, send text messages, take photos, and make calls. They are cloud computing.

The New Normal

Cloud computing is becoming a permanent way of life, just as cell phones have become the "new normal." Web apps and new wireless devices are leading to structural changes. It's like the big bang that created the heavens, except this one is creating virtual clouds and lots of mini-clouds that support this wave of technology that is just starting to rain down on us.

The New Normal = "Structural Change"...Embrace It!

- ▶ Stagecoaches gave way to the railroad and the Pony Express.
- ▶ The Pony Express gave way to the telegraph to deliver messages.
- ▶ The horse and buggy gave way to the automobile.
- ▶ Candlelight gave way to electricity.
- ▶ Desktop software is giving way to cloud computing.
- ▶ Internet browsers are going to fade away to "apps."

Structural Change Is Permanent

Just ten years ago, who would have thought you would pay $4.35 for a 16-ounce cup of coffee? Yet today, you know and recognize Starbucks as the "new normal" in the way you think about and buy coffee. Starbucks' management has been visionary and a leader in the coffee business. They changed our landscape (literally), with a coffee shop on every corner delivering a high-end quality experience centered on a cup of coffee.

Changes in Your Life

- Your hair starts turning grey in your 30s.

- Your eyesight starts getting worse after you turn 40.

- You used to smoke a pack a day; now you take that many pills a day.

Changes in Your Technology

- You used to make telephone calls from a land line…now you speak a name into your Bluetooth and your wireless phone connects you.

- You read the news from a daily evening newspaper…now you use a mobile device to get news and weather reports twenty-four hours a day.

- You bought stationery and greeting cards to send letters and handwritten notes…now you use e-mail or send a text message.

- You adjusted the rabbit ears to pick up reception on your living room TV…now you watch hundreds of Internet movies and shows on your high-speed mobile phone, iPad, or notebook.

- You picked up a paperback book at the mall to take on vacation… now you power up your Kindle, download *Own the Clouds* and set out for a spot on the beach to read.

Make Way For New Clouds

Are you still trying to figure out if you trust using the local bank's ATM? Did you know you can scan checks and make deposits to your bank account using your smartphone? ATM deposits are becoming obsolete. Like the memo said, you've got to get with the times and when it comes to clouds, they change and move fast.

Buy a computer, cell phone, reader, tablet — just about everything you can think of — in January, and by December of that same year it's "old stuff" already. It's been replaced on store shelves with faster, cheaper and smaller versions. The pace at which software and hardware comes at us is getting faster and faster, and stuff keeps getting smaller and smarter.

Steve Jobs, who was a big supporter of cloud computing, predicted that the personal computer was going to go the way of the farm truck. "It won't disappear but it will be relegated to a niche role by more popular mobile devices like smartphones and tablets."[1]

Encyclopedia Britannica was first published in the late 1700s in Edinburgh, Scotland, and grew over time to a twenty-book set. Since the 1990s, Britannica has been faced with digital and online competition. At one point, their sales force was asked to sell CD-ROMs of information instead of books. Some laughed. These salespeople did not see the future of technology and got left behind. Good thing the company's new owner was a visionary. Today, students can get the Encyclopedia Britannica on sets of DVDs, off the Internet, and from their mobile phones.[2]

The Future of Clouds

Cloud-based technology will reach you from space and touch every corner of the planet. It's a fundamental shift in the way you communicate and get information.

- ✓ More than 50 percent of the world's population is under the age of 30 and they are growing up using clouds.[3]

- ✓ Starting with the 2009 freshman class, Boston College stopped doling out new e-mail accounts to students. The college realized that by the time today's student gets to college, he or she already has e-mail set up.[4]

- ✓ In the U.S., senior citizens and women over 55 are the fastest-growing segment on Facebook.[5]

- ✓ Forty-five percent of hiring managers reported, in a survey conducted by CareerBuilders.com, using social media in their background checks of prospective employees.[6]

- ✓ One out of eight married couples in the U.S. met through social media.[7]

✓ A 2009 U.S. Department of Education study revealed that, on average, online students outperformed those receiving face-to-face instruction.[8]

Children born between 1994 and 2004 are called "Generation Z" (Gen Z).[10] These kids stand uniquely apart from any other living group in the world today. They were born when technology ruled the world! The Internet and mobile phones are as common to them as a baby bottle. These kids are plugged in all the way.

This generation makes up nearly 18 percent of the world's population. Gen Z kids prefer to text their friends rather than pick up the phone to talk. They abbreviate messages instead of spelling out words, which makes me wonder if they even know how to spell.

A few years ago, there was a commercial that told folks, "Don't leave home without it." Now with cloud computing, it's okay to leave home. Go. Leave. Go anywhere you desire. The wearable GPS on your belt clip will notify and bring help if you fall. You are a voice command away from anyone you want to reach. You won't need money, either; all you'll need is a smartphone, a debit or credit card app, and a PIN number. In the near future, you may even see these payment options on signs posted in store windows, on your next hotel check in, or on the menu of your favorite restaurant:

Apps ONLY

No Cash.

No Checks.

Plastic Not Accepted.

Must Wear Shoes and Shirts!

Every time you stop for milk and bread and pay by swiping your plastic card, you're in a cloud. Cell towers, electric grids and data centers are just part of the infrastructure that powers the clouds. Clouds crisscross under the ground and through the airwaves nonstop. Invisible signals are swirling around you like you're in a smoke-filled bar on a Saturday night.

Cloud computing is going to continue to develop, innovate and enhance our lives and how we do business. I'm talking about a *structural change* — not a fad. Not a cycle of events that you will, in the end, abandon and then return to your old ways of doing and thinking. Move over and make way…cloud computing is here to stay.

What's Next?

- Wireless devices will turn on the lights in your home, lock or unlock the doors, dim your tinted windows and set up your bathroom mirror with your calendar, text messages and missed calls while you're brushing your teeth and getting ready for the day.

- Your medications will have a biodegradable, networked chip inside them that will relay data to a machine, which will analyze the dosage and how your body processed it.

- Scientists are mapping forests and wildlife using computers, GPS, video cameras, and sniffing devices. As we get more connected through networks, humans can better understand and live in harmony with the earth.

What does all this technology in the future mean for you and investors who want to take advantage of these opportunities? Today's developments are just the tip of the cloud.

There is still time to identify cloud businesses that are making a fundamental shift in how you do business through wireless devices and Internet applications. I am specifically talking about cloud computing companies that are leading the way.

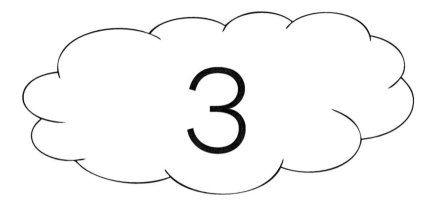

CLOUD REALITIES

"*You can design and create, and build the most wonderful place in the world. But it takes people to make the dream a reality.*"

WALT DISNEY

In the late 1970s Steve Jobs, co-founder of Apple Inc., attempted to get Atari and HP interested in his and Steve Wozniak's ("Woz") computer. It was brand-new technology that came with a vision and visionary developers. Let me share with you what Steve had to say about those proposals he made so many years ago.

"So we went to Atari and said, 'Hey, we've got this amazing thing, even built with some of your parts, and what do you think about funding us? Or we'll give it to you. We just want to do it. Pay our salary; we'll come work for you.' And they said, 'No.' So then we went to Hewlett-Packard, and they said, 'Hey, we don't need you. You haven't got through college yet."[1]

Steve Jobs had the courage to take his idea and keep going until it became what we all know today as Apple. As for Atari, passing up on this opportunity has to be one of their biggest regrets. HP ruled out his ideas because he didn't have a college degree. Please! Some of the most intelligent people I know don't have a college degree.

Clouds – Fashion Statement

I grew up in the era when comic books were popular. One of the best "oldies" was a sci-fi story about Dick Tracy, a detective working for a newspaper. He was known for talking into his watch, called a "two-way wrist radio" — a super high-tech device. It was as far out as you could get.

I got to thinking…had anyone made some twenty-first century version of his talking watch? I Googled "iWatch" and by golly, there it was! An Italian designer is working on a concept similar to the two-way wrist radio. It's a smartphone/wristwatch. The specs include an RSS reader, Wi-Fi and 16GB memory.

What's even more amazing is what else I found — lots of other high-tech fashion statements:

- i-Buckle — wear it on any belt you own.
- i-Ring — a perfect gift for the hard-to-buy-for tech-minded gal or guy.
- i-Neck — a wearable cloud necklace.

I haven't yet found the i-Tie for that special dad on his birthday, but I'm sure it's being developed as I type. Wearable cloud technology is going to be the next big fashion wave. See it for yourself. Do a quick Internet search for the iWatch and see all the other fashions that pop up.

3-D Clouds

A number of companies are coming out with 3-D TVs. Personally, I'm waiting for a hologram 3-D high definition TV (Hol-3-D-TV). When you turn on the nature channel, you won't just watch the elephant cross the Sahara; you'll have to move the coffee table to make room for her to walk by! TV will be a total experience, as if you were right there. It will be interactive. You will be using your hologram TV for phone calls to family and friends.

The hologram TV will make them appear life-size and crystal clear, as if they were sitting across the sofa from you. Your dog can get to know your relative's cat when it strolls into the room.

Personal Avatars

Need a personal assistant (PA)? Before you know it, PA will be short for "personal avatar." An avatar is a computer illustration that resembles you. Some try to mirror the person accurately; others look like a cartoon drawing from a county fair. The younger generation uses avatars when they sign on to the computer to play games, so they can track players.

As technology develops, so will avatars. They will take on a life of their own — your life, to be accurate.

Several computer science graduate students and a professor at Northwestern University's Intelligent Information Laboratory (InfoLab) have developed an automated computer program to comb online news outlets for major stories of the day and pair them with video and still photo.[2] The most interesting part about the newscast is that it's delivered by a virtual woman — an avatar named "Alex."

The future of personal avatars is going to be huge. Your personal avatar will be your virtual assistant. No more answering machines. It will recognize and learn voices. It will be programmed with a full vocabulary on how you speak and it will even have your accent. It will be an extension of your personality. When you are unavailable to answer calls, your PA will step in and actually take over the phone call, explaining in detail, if you like, that you are not able to pick up. Your PA in the future is going to be a virtual you!

Just when you think you've seen it all, your avatar will get a face-lift, a tummy tuck and, if you like, a full makeover…hologram-style. Plastic surgeons start packing your scalpels and looking for a new career! With airbrush technology, you can look taller, younger and you can taper your waist just how you want it without doing sit-ups every day. It's not you in the flesh, but it's the next-best thing.

The flesh part will take a few more years to develop and perfect and will probably happen long after you and I are gone from this life but it will happen someday. With the discovery of organic plastic, infused cloning, and intelligent electronic components, the new-and-improved you is just around the corner. All I can say is, I hope they can program your good looks and quick wit into your avatar!

Business and News Clouds

For years you have asked companies to make monthly bills and quarterly financial statements easier to understand. My vision of a bank or an investment statement is that they "come to life" — even better than the newspapers portrayed in the Harry Potter books and movies where photos of people tell you the news. How neat would it be if your statements — phone bill, electric bill and investment statements — all came with a customer service ava-clone? You open the incoming statement on your TV and the avatar greets you by name and asks if you would like her or him to guide you through your statement. The avatar tells you how much time you spent on your phone or how much electricity you used or how you did in each investment, all the while showing you lovely graphs or bar charts. You can ask it questions and get answers – it's interactive. The avatar is able to show you how you compare with your neighbors in electric usage, how much you made in income and offer you projections for the next twelve months. You can ask the avatar to send tax information directly to your CPA, or pay a bill directly from a voice command. If you just want to say hello or fix a problem, the avatar will notify the company and connect you via their video communication system (VCS).

Cloud power is everywhere you look. Clouds have become a big part of your day in ways our grandparents could never have imagined. With the sound of your voice or by the flick of your finger, you can make devices reach out and touch someone.

Cloud-Based Homes

Cloud power is making your home more efficient and easier to manage. Your home will have high-tech heat and air-conditioning, indoor and outdoor lights and music that turns on and tunes in to your favorite radio stations…all with the touch of a cloud app. You'll be able to cook on your countertop surface without burners, set your oven from a cold position to 350 degrees from your wireless device, or pre-set it the night before to turn on in the afternoon. By the time your family gets home, all the kids have to do is wash up and set the table. Dinner's ready!

Your "smart home" will have a "night" button built into the lighting control switch next to your bed. Press the button and your home system closes the drapes or turns the tinting on your windows dark before turning off all the interior lights. Your smart home system will lock all the outside doors, turn the heater up or down and make sure the alarm is set. All you have to do is tuck in the kids, read them a story and get a good night's sleep.

The best part is that the cost to own these types of cloud-powered homes, cars and personal devices keeps coming down. It's like those first Texas Instruments calculators. When they first came out, they cost hundreds of dollars and you needed to enroll in a three-month class to figure out how to work them. Today, you can pick up a calculator for less than a cup of coffee. Prices on flat-screen TVs and computers are getting more affordable by the month. As time passes, clouds will touch just about every aspect of your life, all for pennies on the dollar. It really will be as affordable as oxygen — almost free.

History Repeats

It was the best of times, it was the worst of times.[3] This was written more than one hundred fifty years ago by Charles Dickens in his novel, A Tale of Two Cities. Ironically, this classic quote easily applies throughout history and today.

In 1929 the Dow Jones Industrial Average (DJIA) opened just above 300. Yale University Professor of Economics Irving Fisher, who was well-respected by Wall Street at the time, made this statement about the stock market: "Stocks have reached what looks like a permanently high plateau."[4] He saw something looming over the economy that would stop the world as he knew it — the Great Depression. During this period in time many companies and banks closed. The U.S. economy struggled for decades. It took time, hard work, and faith in each other to get our country back on its feet. Thankfully, the Dow broke through Professor Fisher's prediction in 1954 and hasn't looked back.

The worst of times came in the form of the 2009 recession. It exposed financial institutions and banks to huge losses from subprime loans that could not be repaid by borrowers. What was seen as a new record for U.S. bank closures in 2008 became even more alarming when that annual figure was exceeded in just the first three months of 2009.[5]

The 2009 recession weakened our automobile industry. Car sales declined to one of their worst periods in two decades, forcing massive layoffs and factories to close their doors. It upset housing and construction. Businesses owners worried, and their employees couldn't help but feel the pressure of reduced work, job losses, and economic uncertainty. High unemployment, home foreclosures, short sales, and bankruptcies became a new reality.

Still, today, professors and economists are calling for the worst of times. They could be right, and they could be wrong. Not that long ago, a prediction was made that got a lot of media attention. "The world would end on May 21, 2011." It didn't! The person who made this forecast was on the news later that day saying his math was off, and that the world would be ending five months later. If you are reading Own the Clouds any time after November 1, 2011 — we are still here! Our country, economy, world stock markets, visionary companies, and new and evolving technology are all still making daily advances — and you are that much older.

The best of times is coming out of this economic turmoil and will open up a vast number of opportunities through cloud computing companies. For those with the ability and willingness to reinvent themselves and embrace new technology, the sky's the limit.

Cloud-Related Jobs

The number of direct and indirect jobs supported by Internet-related activities is on the rise. Internet advertising is now factored into the total U.S. gross domestic product (GDP).

Based on Amazon's 2010 Annual Report, they spent over $2.5 billion on outbound shipping costs.[6] Packages sold by e-tailers (Internet retail companies) are generally shipped by the U.S. Postal Service or one of the major private delivery services. As U.S. Postal Service Manager of Package Services James Cochrane said, "Six years ago, people were pointing at the Internet as the doom and gloom of the Postal Service, and in essence what we've found is the Internet has ended up being the channel that drives business for us."[7]

There is a great lesson to be learned and realize here. If the "big government" U.S. Postal Service can measure the increases in their business as a direct result of the Internet, I can't help but believe that so can astute business owners and job seekers fresh out of college.

In a study released in 2009, the Interactive Advertising Bureau (IAB) cited that Internet-related jobs employ more than 1.2 million Americans with above-average wages in jobs that did not exist two decades ago, and another 1.9 million people work to support those with directly Internet-related jobs. A total of 3.1 million Americans are employed thanks to the interactive ecosystem[8] of the Internet.

Do a search in your web browser for "Salary Snapshots for Web Designers and Developers." Based on national salary data, these jobs start in the low-thirty-thousand range. Add in the bonus and profit-sharing packages, and annual salaries climb into the mid seventy thousands.[9] For two-income families, this could easily add up to a six-figure income. Not too shabby for a young industry. Cloud-related jobs may require learning new job skills, but like anything new, once you get the hang of it, you're good to go.

Cloud Markets

Web-based cloud computing and markets are expanding. N. Chandrasekaran, chief executive of Tata Consultancy Services (TCS), India's largest software company, was quoted in the Daily News & Analysis as saying, "Within the next five years, we hope to get at least a billion dollars" from offering cloud computing to small and medium businesses.[10]

Microsoft is totally committed to cloud computing. In 2011, 90 percent of their 40,000 engineers were working on cloud-related products and services. Steve Ballmer, CEO of Microsoft, told Forbes.com, "The cloud is revolutionizing computing by linking the computing devices people have at hand to the processing and storage capacity of massive data centers, transforming computing from a constrained resource into a nearly limitless platform for connecting people to the information they need, no matter where they are or what they are doing." They will invest $9.5 billion in research and development – more than any other company in the world — solely devoted to cloud technology.[11]

A Day Made of Glass

World-recognized theoretical physicist Dr. Michio Kaku said, "The video revolution is a landmark in the evolution of our species."[12] To get a good sense of the coming wave of cloud technology in your everyday life, I recommend watching "A Day Made of Glass." This is a short video produced by Corning showing how intelligent glass is making its way into your bedroom, bathroom, kitchen, car, office, shopping mall and much more. You can find this video on their home page www.corning.com or on YouTube. This video is amazing. You are going to love it and will want to share it with your family and friends. Peer into your future — peer into the future of clouds.

Every tech company wants to survive and thrive. To do so, they will have to develop web-based technology (cloud computing) with a passion. They will have to figure out how to price their services and products. They will need to stay on the cutting edge or end up on the cutting room floor. One thing is for sure: the web is a very even playing field. The best companies will stand out. Visionary leaders from big or small companies have an equal opportunity to lead us into the next era of cloud computing.

PART II:

A PATHWAY INTO CLOUDS

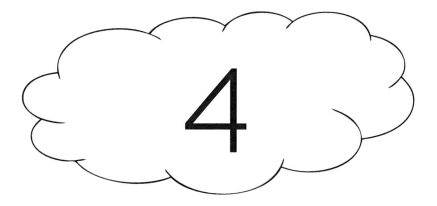

GLOBAL CLOUDS
CONNECT

"Somehow I can't believe that there are any heights that can't be scaled by a man who knows the secrets of making dreams come true."

WALT DISNEY

Webster's dictionary defines a visionary as a "dreamer."[1] Some would call a visionary impractical or unrealistic. That may be true in some cases, but not all. I'm going to define a visionary company as one that sees the possibilities and goes about turning them into everyday realities. Corporate America has bestowed a new title on their movers and shakers who are taking companies in a general direction to develop and enhance their corporate vision. These new business executives are called chief visionary officers (CVOs).

In the world of wireless devices, all the new gadgets and gizmos that will power them will be the inspiration of the next big visionary ideas coming down the road — or out of the clouds. These ideas are coming from the new, innovative companies you'll hear about six months from now. These companies are without borders or boundaries because clouds have no limit and roam free.

Clouds — East and West

Global partnerships and business ventures are forming around the world to develop software and hardware that powers the clouds. By joining together they are solving a larger set of business problems. There is no doubt in my mind that if you can think of a good idea that would improve your cloud experience, someplace on the planet, visionary developers have models or some kind of a prototype already in the works!

Young people around the world have the potential to embrace global capitalism and global technology. The early adopters, those who just have to have the latest and greatest hot-off-the-shelf stuff, raced to stores to get the new generation of Apple's iPad in April 2011. Apple said it sold more iPad 2 devices on its first day than they sold of the original iPad three years earlier over a two-day period.[2]

The 2010 population of China was estimated at more than 1/4 of the world's total population.[3] A 2009 study revealed that China had more Internet users than the entire population of the United States.[4] Chinese kids and young adults are obsessed with the Internet. When you look at China and India in terms of their population and spending power, it becomes clear that they are a force to be taken seriously.

China Mobile, the world's largest wireless operator, estimated in February 2010 that China would have more than 850 million mobile phone subscribers by the end of 2010. They also projected that mobile Internet users would increase 62.5 percent in 2010 to 372.8 million, with prospective growth rate remaining high through 2014.[5] This adds up to more Chinese buying smartphones and other entertainment-enabled phones, laptops, and PCs. In other words, "big bucks" are going to be spent on cloud computing devices of all types.

China's one-party government actively promotes the Internet for business and education. Their rapid rise in web use has helped drive global economic growth (which some sources say reached nearly 10 percent in 2010)[6] in the aftermath of the global recession.

Today, China is looking for ways to reduce its carbon footprint, and cloud computing could very well be a factor in this goal in that it may eventually influence traffic patterns in big cities. According to a recent InformationWeek report, telecommuting — working from home using cloud-based applications — is one of 15 green technology innovations that is having a significant impact by reducing the number of cars on the road.[7]

2010 Data on China

- One out of every three Chinese spends about 18.3 hours online every week, or 2.61 hours each day, on the Internet.
- By the end of 2010, 457 million Chinese were surfing the Internet — a 19 percent jump over 2009.
- China has more than 53 million bloggers.
- Chinese are shopping, banking and paying bills online.[8]

When you look at the citizens of developing countries like China and India, you have to wonder what they will purchase. You know from the news that the people of China are good savers, putting away about 40 percent of their wages. Wouldn't it just make good sense, when they are ready to purchase their first (or second or third) tech item like a cell phone or other device to access the Internet, that they will want a good value… just like you?

The next step is to determine which type of item these consumers will buy and which companies will provide the hardware, software and service plans. It will take time and insight to determine which companies are going to lead this revolution. Financial firms spend hours doing technical analysis along with some good old-fashioned "kicking the tires" kind of work trying to figure this out. They are always on the lookout for visionary companies making new discoveries — the ones laying the foundation of our future.

NOTE: If you should decide to invest in a foreign company, keep in mind there are more risks investing in overseas firms. There are the currency exchange risks and political risks, just to name two areas investors need recognize. There is no guarantee of future performance when investing in foreign or domestic stocks. My recommendation is to check with an experienced financial advisor who can guide you to what's best for you.

Safety — Cyber Crime

Last August, I was flying home from a conference and flipping through *Sky Mall* magazine. I was not surprised to see the RFDI Travel Wallet, a hack-proof wallet. This wallet prevents someone who is holding a radio-wave scanner from stealing your name and address off your passport or driver's license as you walk through the airport terminal, or any place for that matter. You may have seen the term RFID (Radio-Frequency IDentification), which refers to a tiny micro chip or bar code that is embedded with information — in this case, your information! Cyber punks using scanners are able to access your name, credit card numbers, and where you live just by using this snooping technology.

You can never be too careful when it comes to protecting your identity.

You read and hear in the news just about every day that cyber crime is on the rise. Organized online criminal networks along with unhappy groups are hitting from all sides. Hackers are getting more and more sophisticated by the day.

To stop this threat countries and companies are coming together to form security alliances to share information. Safety is critical to cloud computing. If you sense any type of danger, you will stop spending money online. If you did this, cloud company profits would drop, and they could even go out of business. Once you own stock in a cloud company, a breach in their security would definitely not be a good thing. Cloud companies know this. They are making every effort known to man and science to make sure your information is guarded, your cloud shopping is a good experience, and your cloud services are delivered as timely and as safely as possible. Cloud companies understand that your protection is important to growing their businesses and have made your safety their primary concern.

Cloud computing companies need to take a lesson from the most prolific businesses in America: the insurance industry and fast-foods companies. Cloud computing companies need to be *safe, fast, affordable, and easy to use.*

Safe

- ► If you don't feel safe using the Internet for banking, you won't use it.

- ► If you don't feel safe storing your files in data centers, you won't use them.

- ► If you are concerned that opening an e-mail will infect your computer, you won't open it.

- ► If for a minute you had a glimmer of doubt that the online travel site you were using to buy airline tickets would double or triple-charge your account because of a computer glitch, the deal would be off!

- ► If you were concerned that buying a book on Amazon would cause you to have problems with your bank card — or worse, that someone would steal your identity, you would never put yourself in that position.

- ► When you know you're safe, you won't think twice because it will become second nature to you to shop and do your banking online.

- ► When you feel safe you are good to go. But when you don't, you won't make a move.

- ► When you know you are safe you can go ahead and buy from Amazon. Why? Because your information is protected, and so are you.

I wrote a blog last year about Internet security in which I discussed how Internet security was viewed by the U.S. government and our military. Basically, they have done the equivalent of posting a sign on the Internet that reads,

"U.S. GOVERNMENT — NO TRESPASSING."

Computer Fraud and Abuse

The Computer Fraud and Abuse Act is a law that was passed by Congress in 1986 with the sole intention of reducing federal and financial institutions' computer-related offenses. This act has been updated a number of times (1988, 1994, in 2001 by the Patriot Act, 2006, and in 2002 and 2008 by the Identity Theft Enforcement and Restitution Act). There is no doubt in my mind the act will continue to be updated as time goes on.

Internet security benefits everyone. Since private companies are creating the clouds, it just makes sense that they monitor and police themselves and put protections in place to safeguard our information. A joint effort needs to take place between our government and the private sector to keep you safe and, in fact, they are working toward that very end. On May 29 2009, President Obama addressed the American public about the Internet and its role in our nation's economy and daily life.

"From now on, our digital infrastructure, the networks and computers we depend on every day will be treated as they should be; as a strategic national asset. Protecting this infrastructure will be a national security priority. We will ensure that these networks are secure, trustworthy, and resilient. We will deter, prevent, detect, and defend against attacks and recover quickly from any disruptions or damage."[9]

Cyber Policy

One month after President Obama spoke with the nation about our digital future, the White House released the Cyber Space Policy Review. In it they said:

"Cyberspace touches practically everything and everyone. It provides a platform for innovation and prosperity and the means to improve general welfare around the globe. But with the broad reach of a loose and lightly regulated digital infrastructure, great risks threaten nations, private enterprises, and individual rights. The government has a responsibility to address these strategic vulnerabilities to ensure that the United States and its citizens, together with the larger community of nations, can realize the full potential of the information technology revolution."[10]

Our new digital world needs to have basic rules we can all follow, just like the rules we follow every time we get behind the wheel of a car. You are okay to move about the Internet as long as you are not putting others in jeopardy.

The U.S. government is spending billions on Internet projects across 27 different agencies — $77.5 billion was spent in 2010 and $80 billion will be spent in 2011.[11]

World governments and private/public companies are developing technology and constantly looking for ways to make our web travels safer.

It's kind of like designing and building cars. Early cars didn't have seat belts. You still got from place to place without them, but today you know that wearing a seat belt when you drive is a safer way to travel — and it's the law. Using a seat belt saves lives. Internet security will continue to evolve as well, making the Internet super highway safer.

Governments and cloud companies are continually working to keep you safe and worry-free. It will be an ongoing process. It will take time and money. You can be sure cloud companies and world governments will continue to put safeguards in place for themselves and for you.

Peace of Mind

Once you are confident that measures are in place to protect you and your information, the next three components that need to be in unison are: a fast response time, right pricing, and that it's *easy* to use.

Fast

- If you have to wait for what seems like hours for your computer to move from site to site, you'll get frustrated and stop using the service.

- If your computer responds with quick reflexes, it will become second nature to surf the web for news, stock quotes and shopping.

Affordable

- If you pay a flat rate that's reasonable, you'll buy into a service and keep it.

- If you can save money using a cloud based service, you will buy online.

According to J.D. Power and Associates, "Travelers made 70 percent of travel reservations online in 2008, up from 55 percent in 2007."[12] They attribute this to convenience, the perception that booking online saves money and because it's safe!

Easy to Use

- When it's easy to use, you are good to go.

I purchased my first Internet/TV service in 2011 for a one-time fee of $29.95. I access satellites via my Internet connection and get more than 3,500 TV channels from every country in the world. Let me tell you what I really purchased for less than thirty dollars: I bought **IP addresses** that connect to specific satellites. When I click on a show or broadcast to watch, the service connects me to the fixed IP address and starts streaming the show right to my laptop or iPad. I get sports, news, movies, TV shows, music and business channels in the comfort of my home or out in a public Wi-Fi spot. As long as you know the IP address of the satellite from which your source is broadcasting, you can connect and do the same, thereby allowing you to bypass most cable and satellite services. In my case, I weighed the value of my time. Looking up 3,500 IP addresses versus paying an affordable one-time fee — which makes more sense? Your time and my time are a lot more valuable than trying to access all that information ourselves.

I love the fact that I don't have to pay a monthly fee, that there was no hardware to install, and that I have access twenty-four hours a day, every day. When an IP address changes, my cloud service merely updates it for me. I don't do a thing…all I needed was a way to connect to the clouds (the Internet).

Safe, fast, affordable, and easy to use — everything you want and look for in **cloud computing**.

7 WAYS TO KEEP YOUR DEVICES SAFE

1. Install anti-spyware and anti-malware on your computer and make sure they're activated and up-to-date.

2. Keep passwords in a secure place. If you're on the clouds, use a

password "double encryption" site for your data. I recommend using a cloud computing company that is located in the country of your origin. If you are in the U.S. use a data center facility housed in America. You don't want to run the risk of a foreign government seizing your data in an act of war.

3. Put your devices up and away from little kids and pets. Keep them out of the hot sun in the summer. Keep your devices dry. If you love water sports, there are several good waterproof cases on the market you can use. (Ladies: cleavage is not a waterproof storage compartment for your phone, and a blow dryer won't fix the problem.)

4. Buy a remote for your cell phone that beeps if you walk away and leave it. If you carry your phone on your belt, make sure that when you get out of the car, it's still on you.

5. Travelers may want to consider buying a solar panel charging kit. They make them for your cell phone, laptop and notebook. Do a web search for: "Solar Laptop Charger Kits."

6. Purchase a low-cost insurance policy to repair or replace your device in case it is damaged or stolen.

7. Keep your computer clean from the inside out. Get a computer professional to clean the food, hair, dust and gunk off your computer. While he is at it, have him run a cleaning program to clean up the inside. Your computer and laptop will run cooler and faster.

7 WAYS TO KEEP YOUR DATA SAFE

1. Go with a reputable vendor to back up and store your data. They will have security in place that will slow down and hopefully prevent foreign or domestic hackers.

2. Look for a vendor that has strong passwords. Keywords to look for are "authentication" and "authorization." Your data must be

encrypted as it goes back and forth.

3. Ask your cloud vendor to make data file transfers only to authorized devices.

4. Ask if they offer an "auto-erase" if your data is compromised by an unauthorized employee gone rogue!

5. Businesses storing data in clouds need to check that the vendor is compliant with privacy laws.

6. While your main reasons for cloud-based storage are backups and archiving data, this is not a substitute for a formal audit trail. Check with the vendor before you sign up for their services and ask what they offer to back up sensitive information. Then make sure the audit trails within the service are backed up onto your system.

7. If your cloud vendor comes under attack and shuts off service, you need to have a plan in place and know what to do. You may even need a disaster recovery plan.

CLOUDS ON THE GROUND

"Biggest problem? Well, I'd say it's…MONEY. It takes a lot of money to make these dreams come true."

WALT DISNEY

$1.6 Million Bet

One Sunday afternoon in 1999 Jeff Taylor, CEO of Monster.com, decided to place a bet on the Super Bowl. He didn't bet on which team would win the football game. Nope. He bought a thirty-second commercial, "When I Grow Up" and paid $1.6 million to air it! Today it's a classic, and it went like this:

> "…When I grow up I want to file. When I grow up I want to be under-appreciated. When I grow up I want to be forced into an early retirement…"

In a twenty-four-hour period following the ad's run, Monster's website hits soared from 83,000 to 2.2 million, and the number of résumés posted on the site went from a typical 1,500 a day to 8,500 on the Monday following the game.[1]

Monster had set up a very high-tech, expensive, multi-server computer center to handle all this Internet traffic. It paid off and Taylor has made millions. Back then, that was how it was done. There were no data centers he could rent space from for those seasonal peak times. His only option was to invest a bunch of money in software, hardware and people to run it.

Today his options would be a lot different. He could rent server space from a virtual source for peak needs instead of spending thousands to service this in-house.

Software or *Cloud*-ware

Ever had your computer freeze up on you? Have you ever ended up staring at a blank screen in the middle of the day, and no matter what you tried, your computer would just not do anything? You are not alone. As you save more and more stuff on your hard drive, your computer's response time gets slower, or worse, it crashes. If this happens, you could lose everything you've spent years saving.

As you fill up your computer memory with large files like photos, music, video and games, you have to decide whether to buy a larger storage device that sits on the floor to hold all your stuff, or store your data in the clouds. A good-size storage device can cost from a few hundred dollars to thousands of dollars. If you're like me, you'll hire an IT person to set it up and transfer your data, which costs more money. Storing your data in the clouds is cost effective, since what you pay is based on how much data you store. Just like the corner public storage unit down the street from your home, you pay for how much space you need. A couple of clicks and it's set up and done. You save major headaches — not to mention your time and money — because your data is always there.

As a businesswoman, I know firsthand that once your software manufacturer stops supporting your older software version of their program, it's time to upgrade. I bought a software program for my financial services business in 1986. Back then, it came on a five-inch floppy disk. The program ran on the DOS operating system, which has long been abandoned for a Windows version. I still use the software. I've had to upgrade it probably five or six times over the years, and I need to upgrade it again. This time I am going with a cloud-based web version. I won't spend $900 on software to download to my office computers. My data will be stored and will come to me via the clouds from data centers. The web version will run me $30 for a one-time fee and $2.50 a month. The savings are truly amazing.

Tapping into cloud-ware, a web application (cloud computing) offers the same software virtually (in the clouds) and costs just pennies a day. Virtual software is accessed from the Internet. It's a web application you can open from any place in the world as long as you have a device like a laptop, smartphone or iPad and an Internet connection or Wi-Fi.

Spam: Food or Junk Mail?

Ever eaten Spam? Know what it is? It's food — a pork product on the salty side and very tasty with pineapple on top. Ask a person under 30 if she's ever eaten Spam, and she'll look at you like you are nuts. Everyone under 30 knows that spam is junk mail.

If you have an e-mail account, you've received spam. More importantly, you've also been cloud computing. E-mail is virtual! The information is transmitted to you remotely. It comes from a cloud "up above." It comes from a data center.

Data Centers

Cloud computing has roots in physical locations called, data centers where data is stored and transmitted. Data centers house millions and billions of bits and bytes of information. These state-of-the-art, air-conditioned warehouses and shipping containers are lined up and stacked up, and are filled with computer servers ready to transmit data on demand.

Data centers are becoming a new online utility, just like water and electricity are now. Data centers don't power down. Servers are never turned off! Just like your electric light switch, they are waiting and ready – every day.

To get a good idea of what a data center is all about, do a YouTube search for "Google data center." This is a tour of their facility and is very interesting.

The Shift to Data Centers

Computer crashed? Lost all your files! I had a really close call and that was enough to make me a believer in backing up my data. I know what you're thinking, because I've been down that road myself. You're thinking you'll go out and buy a server or a backup drive and put it next to your computer. Your data will be safe. Maybe. At any time, you could be wiped out by a fire and overhead sprinklers could drench your system, ruining it beyond repair. It happens all the time. If you lose your server or backup drives from whatever happened to destroy them, you're toast! You will spend hours upon hours — not to mention thousands of dollars — re-creating the lost data.

Storing your data in the clouds (data centers) takes a good chunk of worry off your shoulders. If you need the data, it's accessible anytime and from any place — your home, office or hotel when you're traveling. You improve your disaster recovery backup plan and sleep better for pennies on the dollar.

Selecting a Data Center

Here's some food for thought when you're looking for a data center. Find a company that charges a fair amount for their service based on the amount of data you'll be storing with them. You want a company that will be around when you need your data. You need to know they are viable and profitable. You also want to know where the data centers are located. If you are in the U.S., have your data centers located in the U.S. Also ask the company if they have more than one backup site.

At the Consumer Electronics Show I asked a major vendor who was promoting a cloud-based application, "Who does the data belong to — the person or the data center?" The vendor didn't have an answer for me. My concern is if you store your data with a foreign company and for some reason they decide all data belongs to them, where does that leave you? I strongly recommend using data center from the country you live and work in — preferably a provider with more than one location to store data.

Public Clouds

Public data centers (public clouds) are open for everyone to use on a shared basis, like the Google data center. They are secure and allow you to store and connect to your data. Once you are connected to the Internet, public clouds allow you to remotely give and receive data from your home, office, car, boat — just about everywhere. Hot spots offer Wi-Fi connections, like at the corner coffee shop.

Private Clouds

Private clouds are the most secure and the most costly. These offer individual servers that large corporations own the exclusive right to use, and have the ability to store and retrieve data on demand. Private clouds are used by major corporations like banks, insurance companies, financial services firms and hospitals. Governments also use them to store their data. It saves them money in the long run since they don't have to maintain the servers. They don't need to hire a department of technicians to keep them up and running. If there is a breakdown, the data center staff is responsible to get it fixed or move your information to a server that is working properly. They are also less dependent on traditional hardware, such as personal computers.

Four Private Cloud Options

1. **Dedicated servers**. Large corporations can contract with a data center to own a set number of servers dedicated to just that customer.

2. **Dedicated hosting**. Customers can rent space in physical servers.

3. **Hybrid hosting**. A combination, where businesses have a set number of dedicated servers they own and additional servers they rent on demand.

4. **Cloud hosting**. Renting on demand or by the hour.

Private – Take-Out

Do you know what day of the year is the biggest for pizza orders? This honor falls on Super Bowl Sunday! Today, a national pizza company can rent from a private data center for those seasonal times when orders spike. This keeps their web site from crashing and orders flowing. They don't have to go out and buy a warehouse of computer servers housed in an air-conditioned facility for those one or two peak days a year. They save money and time and we eat lots of pizza! It's a perfect plan if you ask me.

Four Cloud Observations

1. The ability to access information around the clock from cloud computing companies will come from a variety of service providers.

2. The number of servers needed to hold all this data is going to grow as more information is produced and stored in the clouds.

3. Electrical power usage will creep up as data centers pop up to meet the needs of cloud-based technology.

4. Using "Green Clouds," those devices that produce a smaller electrical footprint, may be rewarded with tax credits, rebates, low-interest loans and other incentives for large-scale businesses and consumers to use.

SIFTING THROUGH CLOUDS

"I always like to look on the optimistic side of life, but I am realistic enough to know that life is a complex matter."

WALT DISNEY

Let me ask you, where were you the morning of March 13, 1986? I can tell you exactly where I was and what I was doing. I was working as a financial advisor for a major Wall Street firm. I had been making client calls that morning to offer up 100 shares for a brand-new tech stock that was about to make its public début, or, as we in the business refer to it, its initial public offering (IPO).

I made dozens of calls offering this new stock. It's not easy trying to explain a software company to folks who don't own a computer and are just barely comfortable using an ATM at their bank. It was like pulling teeth. So I came up with an example to try and explain "software" and came up with *underwear*! Yep, it's true. I still shake my head…what was I thinking? But it worked and went something like this:

Most of us wear underwear. It's how we start our day. No one sees them and we assume everyone has on a pair. (My mom always said to be sure and put on a clean pair in case I was ever in an accident.)

Now, compare this to software. Your computer "wears" software. Under all the layers of developer codes, it's there. It's part of operating your computer day-to-day. No one sees the actual software, like your undies. I assume we all have on a clean, nice-looking pair. At night when you turn your computer off, it goes to sleep. The next day, you turn it back on and *voila*! It's fresh and ready to go again.

Only a couple of folks wanted to buy a "software" (a.k.a. "underwear") company. Who knew back then that this was the beginning of a huge shift — a *structural change*.

Looking back is easy. Looking forward is like gazing into a crystal ball or at tea leaves. If you knew the outcome, you would have jumped in with both feet, or at the very least taken a leap of faith. Did you see the changes that were coming out of new technology? Some investors did and others didn't. The stock was Microsoft.

From an IPO price of $21 back in 1986, to nine stock splits as of August 2011, those initial one hundred shares have now multiplied to 28,800 shares. I'll let you pull up the price of Microsoft (MSFT) and figure out just how much a two thousand one hundred dollar initial investment would be worth today.

The great and powerful Oz, Ray Ozzie, is the former chief software architect at Microsoft, drove much of their early cloud computing work. He was heralded by Bill Gates as one of the world's great programmers. Mr. Ozzie wrote a memo to the entire Microsoft company in 2005. The subject was, "The Internet Services Disruption." Keep in mind this was just after the dot-com bubble burst. In this now famous memo, he talked about being in an exciting time, and that their company was at a new beginning — possibly the biggest new product cycle in their history. This was well before the term "cloud computing" was coined. He called for great changes and that Microsoft needed to reflect on their core strategy and direction.[1]

How do you as an investor find the next big cloud computing company? There are several thousand actively traded tech companies on U.S. stock exchanges. This is a lot of tech to sift through. Before you begin searching for cloud computing companies, you'll need to understand the difference between an "industry" and a "sector" of the market and then you'll want an edge in the market to put it all together.

Industry and Sector of the Market

An **industry** is a group of companies doing the same type of work. Examples of industries are:

- The software industry
- The hardware industry
- The telecommunications industry

Now, put them all together and you have a sector of the market.

Technology Sector

Here is a listing and then a quick overview of each of the groups that comprise the general technology sector.

1. Communications Equipment

2. Computer Hardware

3. Computer Networking

4. Computer Peripherals

5. Computer Services

6. Computer Storage Devices

7. Electronic Instruments and Controls

8. Office Equipment

9. Scientific and Technical Instruments

10. Semiconductors

11. Software and Programming

Communications Equipment

You talk — they make it happen. This sector provides services that enable the delivery of communications and data services across networks globally. Their services connect local and long-distance providers, international service providers, cable operators, voice and data. They also design and manufacture cell phones and satellite systems, along with other hardware for communication systems.

Computer Hardware

These companies do the heavy lifting. They make all the toys and gadgets we use, like digital media players, electronic notebooks, readers, and tablets. Just about anything you can drop and break, these guys make it.

Computer Networking

These are the companies that bring us all together on the Internet and make life much easier to give and get information. Computer networking is the glue of cloud computing. This group provides the technology that delivers shared applications. I'm referring to web conferences as well as remote technical support, Internet security, data storage devices, voice and speech automation, standard web browsing, web file transfers and e-mail.

Computer Peripherals

Pointing devices, keyboards, desktops, webcams, speakers, headsets, and presentation tools — I call this the "other stuff" we add to enhance our cloud computing experience.

Computer Services

This is where computer guys and gals can shine! They help control and collect billions of pieces of data and spit it back on demand. These folks have the magic wand to make it happen for you and me. They fix hardware problems and keep computer systems running smoothly.

Computer Storage Devices

These companies store and archive data like your e-mails, favorite web pages, images, reports and records. Storing your files in the clouds allows you to get at your files quickly, and the data is encrypted to add a layer of security.

NOTE: A quick word about encryption. **Don't forget your password!** It's not like calling a locksmith for help. Internet data storage and password protection is airtight. If you forget your password you're out of luck and locked out of your data.

Electronic Instruments and Controls

These companies design, make, and sell electronic products for information and telecommunications systems — ATMs, power plants, elevators, railway vehicles, medical equipment, power tools, construction machinery and automotive industries.

Office Equipment

This group makes and sells printers, copiers, fax machines, ink products, scanners and all kinds of equipment used in offices. This is the same group that made manual and electric typewriters.

Scientific and Technical Instruments

This group designs, develops and makes high-precision equipment for life sciences, communications, and electronics, as well as chemical, medical and optical companies.

Semiconductors

Chips, chips, and more chips! Semiconductors are the heart of the microprocessor chips that run our electronic devices.

Software and Programming

Software and programming (like the operating system Windows – a.k.a. "underwear") are the road maps that guide and direct your devices when you turn them on. They are made from millions of codes running invisibly behind your computer screen. Software and programming sent a man to the moon and missions to Mars!

Yahoo — Technology Sector List

You are going to need to know how to find and check out cloud computing companies. To get you started, I suggest using **Yahoo Finance**. It's easy to use, and the price is right – it's free. **Yahoo Finance [Sectors] Technology**

Here is the link: http://biz.yahoo.com/p/8conameu.html

The Yahoo technology sector is broken down into thirty-two subgroups.

Industry

Application Software
Business Software and Services
Communication Equipment
Computer-Based Systems
Computer Peripherals
Data Storage Devices
Diversified Communication Services
Diversified Computer Systems
Diversified Electronics
Healthcare Information Services
Information and Delivery Services
Information Technology Services
Internet Information Providers
Internet Service Providers
Internet Software and Services
Long-Distance Carriers
Multimedia and Graphics Software
Networking and Communication Devices
Personal Computers
Printed Circuit Boards
Processing Systems and Products
Scientific and Technical Instruments

Security Software and Services
Semiconductor - Broad Line
Semiconductor - Integrated Circuits
Semiconductor - Specialized
Semiconductor - Equipment and Materials
Semiconductor - Memory Chips
Technical and System Software
Telecom Services - Domestic
Telecom Services - Foreign
Wireless Communications

Click on the hyperlink for [**Application Software**] and you'll be sent to a new page. **Sectors > Technology > Application Software**

Click on: **(More Info)**.You will be redirected to a **Summary** page for **Application Software**.

To dig deeper into this sector, on the left side of the page you'll see: **More On This Industry**

- **Summary** (This is the page you are currently viewing).

- **Leaders & Laggards**

- **Company Index**

- **Industry Browser**

When you click on [**Company Index**] you'll get an alphabetized list of all the public and private/foreign companies that make up this group. You'll have the ability to download and save a list of these companies into spreadsheets to sort and work on later.

There are a number of industries related to clouds that you won't find under the tab [**Technology**]. One sector you won't find under technology that's totally internet based is e-tailers (Internet retail companies). They will be listed under "**Retail**."

Survival of the Fittest

For every one hundred companies that develop the newest gadget or gizmo, only a handful will survive and fewer will make it big. As an investor, you will want to be on the lookout for those select cloud companies that have the ability to do well over time.

Before you invest your hard-earned money, revisit these questions I brought to your attention in Chapter 1 for each cloud company you're considering:

1. Is there a market for the company's products or services?

2. Is there a need for their products or services?

3. Is there a desire for their products or services?

4. Can the company deliver the goods and/or services as promised?

5. What's their track record?

6. Can the company provide value as good as or better than their competitors?

7. Would you buy the company's products or use their services?

8. Would you recommend the company to others and be a repeat customer?

PART III:

THE FOUR KEY CLOUD ELEMENTS

With the help of the Internet and current technology, you can get information on just about anything, including cloud computing. I am going to share with you how I do research using a number of techniques to uncover investment opportunities. I call these the **Four Key Cloud Elements**.

Elements one through three will help you identify potential cloud companies to own. Some cloud computing companies are going to pop into your head. Others won't be so obvious. For now, just keep in mind how they "might fit" into your investment portfolio.

The fourth element is your visual confirmation and, in my opinion, is one of the most critical components to making a decision about cloud computing companies. Being able to recognize a stock trend using charts is a necessary tool every investor must use. Charts take the emotion out of investing. Charts allow you to see how a stock is moving, up and down. I use charts on every buy and sell decision I make, and so should you. I am going to share with you one of my favorite charting tools: Bollinger Bands.

Let's take a moment to look at these four key cloud elements a bit closer up.

The First Key Cloud Element: "Polar Clouds" (highest level)

These are the highest clouds on our planet. As an investor, you want to get the highest vantage point you can when you first start looking for cloud computing companies. You want to be able to look out over all the publicly traded companies to find those that stand out above the rest. You want to identify the "big cloud" computing companies below.

The Second Key Cloud Element: "Cirrus Clouds" (high level)

These are ice-particle clouds, at an average of five or more miles above the earth. They appear as a fine, whitish veil, produce a halo phenomenon when between the observer and the sun or moon.[1] Often, investors tend to focus on just those super-sized, big-name companies and can miss out on clouds located in different sectors of the market. This element is going to help you lift the veil and look down using search engines, bloggers, newsletters and e-zines.

The Third Key Cloud Element: "Stratus Clouds" (mid level)

These clouds give off water droplets and through them you can see both the sun and the moon. The third key element is going to take you behind the scenes to do some reverse engineering. You'll see how companies are spending their cash. You'll see what their management, officers and directors are doing with their shares, from an inside perspective. You'll see how many shares of stock company insiders are buying or selling. As an investor it is important to know this before you get in or out (buy or sell) of a position.

The Fourth Key Cloud Element: "Cumulus Clouds" (low level)

These low-lying clouds tend cover the entire sky. When blue sky does peek through, it looks like breaks in these clouds. Just like these low-altitude clouds, knowing what to look for in a stock chart can be the break you need as an investor. Charts take the emotion out of your investment decisions. They provide you with a picture showing a trend developing or changing in the price movement of a stock. You need to be aware of these trends and be able to recognize patterns. This fourth key cloud element is a critical step you cannot skip.

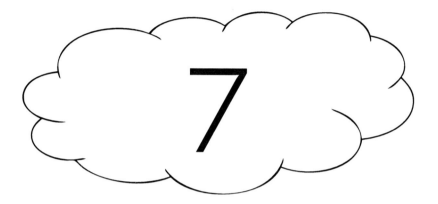

POLAR CLOUDS

SKY-HIGH

"...an experimental prototype community of tomorrow that will take its cue from the new ideas and new technologies that are now emerging from the creative centers of American industry."

WALT DISNEY

The First Key Cloud Element — Polar Clouds

These are the highest clouds on our planet. As an investor, you want to get the highest vantage point when you first start looking for cloud computing companies. You want to identify the "big cloud" computing companies below.

When I started doing research in 1985, I could call an analyst in my New York office for advice on a stock. On a good day, I'd reach one. More often, I'd hit the books. Our office had a library of Standard & Poor's stock reports. Each stock report was printed on double-sided paper, not quite 8.5x11. I don't remember how many binders held all those reports, but it was a lot. It took somewhere between four and six weeks for each company's sheet to recycle and get updated. These reports were valuable. They compiled critical company information needed to see how things were going.

When you wanted a report, you kept your fingers crossed that the filing was current and that no one swiped the binder or page you needed! If you (the investor) wanted to look at this information, you had to drive to the office, or one of a few libraries or colleges that bought this pricey research. You would sit down and spend hours looking up data and taking handwritten notes. It was a long process to get information compared to what we have today.

With the Internet, you have access to all this research and much more. A good portion of it is free to use and available on demand 24/7. It's literally a click away. It's at your fingertips. No more hunting for binders and tracking down missing pages. It's up-to-date and easy to find.

Paper or Cloud

Polar clouds, your first key cloud element, will help you find cloud businesses that are moving forward from their continued success and strong momentum. They post gains and show profits. They have products, services, patent protections and a visionary management that's not just keeping up, but leading the way.

Start by making a list of all the popular names in technology. My list is called the "cloud core" list. You know these companies by name. They are obvious. You hear about them in the news; they come up in conversations. They are known as visionaries. They are on the leading edge of tech. They have the technology, devices and software everyone else is trying to copy. If you think of them, write their names down. These companies are the 800-pound gorillas in the room. They dominate! They take a big bite out of their competition and market share. Put them on your cloud core list. Don't second-guess yourself. At this point, you are forming an initial lineup.

NEW — Cloud Computing Stock Index

Just as I was ready to hand off *Own the Clouds* to my editor, I received a news alert that an online firm had just announced a new cloud computing stock index. I knew it was just a matter of time before this came about. This index is a composite list of companies in the cloud computing sector, and is a good place to check out to do some of your own research. To view the new cloud index, go to www.Tickerspy.com. Their site led me to another online company. Check out www.Investorideas.com and search for their "Tech Sector Directory." These sites will get you off to a good start with lots of information and ideas you don't want to miss.

Hip Low-Tech

A fundamental approach is when you take a look to see whether a company has strong market share, an edge, or a big advantage with their product or service. A very easy way to start is by checking out what your kids and grandkids are buying and using. Just like fashion, tech is a "must-have" for teenagers. As long as they are happy consumers, you're okay. Just don't get too cozy; fashion and tech change quickly!

Web High-Tech

From this point on, you will be doing searches using a free online service from Yahoo called Yahoo Finance. For some of you, this is like learning a foreign language and it will take some practice. I'm very confident that you will get the hang of this pretty quickly.

As you dig into financials, you can tell a lot about a company. You'll find cloud companies with advantages that allow them to sustain and grow earnings and cash flow. Start by asking two questions to build your "cloud core" list.

1) Does the company dominate its field?

These cloud computing companies have the potential to change how we do everything. Wall Street calls these companies "big dogs." Think Sam Walton and Wal-Mart. He started out as an employee at J.C. Penney in the 1940s. Over time, he bought a five and ten store in Bentonville, Arkansas, that turned into a company called Wal-Mart. Sam Walton had a vision and worked hard. By the early 1990s, it was easy to make the case that his company was a big dog in retail.

Don't confuse big dogs with "dogs of the Dow." That's something very different. The dogs of the Dow theory looks primarily at the Dow Jones Industrial Stock Index (thirty stocks from different market sectors). The dogs of the Dow investment strategy is used to find "value" stocks, or stocks on sale. Their per-share cost is low enough to make the dividend stand out. The theory behind this is that these "dogs," or these five to ten highest-dividend-yielding Dow stocks, need a bath, flea dip and some home-cooked meals to look good again. From a mutt to AKC champion show dog! In essence, that's what they are hoping for in this investment strategy. Cloud companies, for the most part, are going to be "growth" stocks. That said, I've identified cloud computing companies from the dogs of the Dow, so you just never know where you'll find clouds.

Some big-dog cloud stocks may seem pricey. Please don't overlook their potential just because they are not a low-priced stock. They didn't get a high value on their stock for being bad. These are today's winners and potentially tomorrow's, too. If they dominate in their industry, there is a good chance they have the power to continue to surprise and reward you.

Price Earnings Ratio (P/E)

Some of you may be wondering why I am not spending time going over Price Earnings Ratio (P/E Ratio). That is a very good question. Many cloud companies have a high P/E. A low P/E shows a bargain or good "value," like the "dogs of the Dow." When looking for cloud computing companies to invest in, you're not necessarily looking for deep-value stocks that are on sale. That's another topic and another book. You are looking for those companies that are hitting their numbers and growing their business. They can have a high or a low P/E number. Don't let this be a stumbling block in your decisions.

START HERE

In the address bar of your computer, type: **www.yahoo.com**. Select **[Yahoo Finance]** located on the left side column. When the finance page comes up, type a stock symbol in the **GET QUOTES** box to get an overview of the stock.

This overview looks like "**Exhibit No. 1**," which is a mock-up of a **Yahoo Finance "Summary Page"** that I created just for *Own the Clouds*. You will be using this as a point of reference and for instructional purposes. It is not an exact rendering of the Yahoo "Summary Page" you'll see when you pull up a stock quote. Please know this exhibit is not complete or accurate. Yahoo web pages change and improve all the time. It is, however, good enough for what you're going to need. Like Disney, I'm going to show it to you in pictures.

As soon as you open the Yahoo Finance "Summary Page", take a look at the middle top section. (Inside the cloud bubble on Exhibit No. 1.) Key-in on two pieces of information: the **Last Trade** and the **1y Target Est** (one-year target estimate). When you look at this area, you'll see that I have purposely left out all of the other data in this section. As you begin researching, you'll want to get an idea of what the one-year price target estimate is for your cloud based company, which is based on analyst estimates.

In Exhibit No.1, you'll see a double-headed arrow pointing between the **"Last Trade"** and the **"1y Target Est."** This price gap is the difference between what your cloud computing company is selling for now and what it's expected to be priced at a year from now. This gap could be the difference in a potential gain or a loss. It's a guideline to help in your decision-making process.

EXHIBIT No. 1

Own the Clouds

"Summary" Page –Yahoo Finance

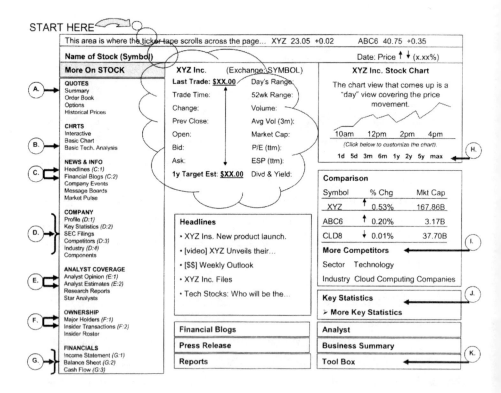

Last Trade – The last price someone paid for shares to buy in, or the sale price someone received for selling shares.

1y Target Est – This dollar figure is the average price per share a group of analysts who cover the stock estimate the price of the shares will be valued at, one year out.

Yahoo Finance — ANALYST COVERAGE > Analyst Opinion

It's time to see what Wall Street folks are saying about your company. I assume you are logged into **Yahoo Finance**, so in the **[GET QUOTES]** box, type in the stock symbol.

Scroll down the left column to **ANALYST COVERAGE** and click on **[Analyst Opinion]**. *(Exhibit No.1, E:1)*

This page is divided into four sections:

1. **Recommendation Summary**

2. **Price Target Summary**

3. **Upgrades and Downgrades History**

4. **Recommendation Trends**

Recommendation Summary is a one-to-five rating scale. If the group consensus is a "strong buy," the recommendation will come back a 1.0. If the group feels the stock is a "sell," the recommendation will come back as a 5.0.

Price Target Summary is a range of prices from a high to a low, an average and the mean target price. These estimates are based on findings from a number of research analysts called brokers. The mean target is what you see on the profile page as the one-year price target that we just discussed. The Price Target Summary is an estimate for one year out. Take a look at what the price target is and how many brokers are in this mix. The low target is a worst-case scenario, and the high target is the best. If you are going to use this as a gauge to buy or sell a stock, I have found the mid range is better than the near-term stock price — if it's not already sitting on it or close to it. I've also noticed from time to time some of the price targets from Yahoo can lag a bit, meaning the analyst estimates may not be as fresh as you'd like. Still, it will give you a range to consider.

Upgrades and Downgrades History An upgrade is when an analyst increases the rating from a "hold' to a "buy" or a "strong buy" on a stock. She feels the price is going to move higher because of some fundamental, technical or industry indicator.

A downgrade is just the opposite. Something in the analyst's research has guided her to lower the rating on the stock to a "hold," "underperform" or "sell."

Major Rating Categories

- Strong Buy
- Buy
- Hold
- Underperform
- Sell

Upgrades and Downgrades History is listed by date and research firm. If you would like a longer list click on the blue hyperlink (below the text box) on this web page; a new window will open a page, showing you an expanded history on upgrades and downgrades.

When you hear or read an analyst say the stock is "overvalued" and being downgraded, what she could be saying is that it got ahead of her one-year price estimate and it's time to trim the position (sell some shares). It moved up to the stock's price point and could be out of steam for awhile.

In my past experience working for a major Wall Street firm that provided research reports, it was not uncommon for an analyst to wait before putting a "sell" recommendation on a stock until it was at rock bottom. Instead of a sell rating, an analyst would go for a hold or underperform rating until the darn thing tanked! Why is that, you ask? Let me share with you a true story from my early days in the business.

I phoned our insurance analyst to get his take on selling a stock. A major hurricane was just off the Gulf Coast and headed for land. At the time the insurance company's stock had a "buy" rating on it. He told me he would *not lower the rating*, or put a sell out on the insurance stock, until the hurricane hit land and did damage. After the fact – yes, he would review his analysis and the rating, but not until he knew whether the hurricane had done billions in damage. I was amazed with the stance he took on this stock. The weather reports were absolutely sure this was going to cause major destruction – and it did! Fortunately, I sold the stock before the damage was done. The next day, and after the stock had dropped in value, he came out with a "hold" on the stock.

I learned a very valuable lesson that day to do my own thinking and analysis. Looking back now, I realize he did me a huge favor, and one I'm happy to share with you.

Wall Street is a tightly knit community. Everyone knows everybody. The firm and the analyst doing the research want a friendly relationship with the management of the companies they follow. No one wants to tick off management and put a strain on their relationship. A sharp downgrade puts pressure on the stock. With the speed of the Internet and mobile devices, a controversial stock report can hit the airwaves and go global in seconds! Before you know it, angry shareholders are calling and writing the company, and attorneys are filing class action lawsuits. So instead of a sell, an analyst may rate a stock a hold or underperform.

When you do see a sell rating on a stock, take a moment and ask yourself: Could this be a bottom? And at some point in time, do you consider buying or adding to a position? Or, is it time to take some or all of the shares out and move on?

Recommendation Trends Take a look back over the past three months at what's being said, then and now, about a company. As an investor, you want to check the trend before you buy or sell. If I've said this once, I've said it a thousand times: *don't buck a trend*. A trend is your friend. Let me explain. For those of you who watch car races, you know about drafting. This is when you get behind a fast car and their air coming off the back of the car pulls you along. Your car picks up additional speed and, if you're an experienced driver, you can pass the car in front of you. Stock trends get some of their air from upgrades and downgrades. Ideally, you want to own a (cloud computing) stock before it gets upgraded, so you can enjoy the push-up in value.

Yahoo Finance — ANALYST COVERAGE > Research Reports

Often, analysts who follow a company will make on-site visits to their competitors' home offices to ask what they think of the other company. This gives them a different slant and possibly some interesting insights on what they are doing right or wrong. These same analysts produce and sell stock research to private groups and the public. A well-known and respected research firm you may recognize is S&P (Standard & Poor's).

You can pay for research on a company if you find a report that you just have to have. Stock reports can run you from a few dollars into the thousands of dollars. You can pay with a debit or credit card right off their report website and have the data electronically sent to you in a PDF in minutes. There are also newsletters available online. Their content and prices will vary depending on what you are looking for. Much of what you are going to need in the way of research will be right at your fingertips — hot off the Internet and free to use. You can also get a lot of your research from free websites, so don't worry about running up costs at this point.

Yahoo Finance — COMPANY > Competitors

On the main "Summary Page," click on [**Competitors**]. *(Exhibit No. 1, D:3)* Right off the bat, it compares side by side how your company looks next to its toughest competition. It gives you even more ideas and companies to check out. This comparison page looks at a number of indicators for your company and their two or three top competitors. This is a tool you will come back to over the years. Not only can you compare companies in the same niche, you can also see where they fall inside their industry group.

Direct Competitor Comparison

Here's a snapshot of the terms you'll see on the competitors page, and my layman's definition of what they mean.

- **Market Cap (Capitalization)**: This tells you the dollar value of the company based on the total number of shares times its stock price.

- **Employees**: How many are on payroll. This may or may not take into account private contractors.

- **Qtrly Rev Growth (yoy)**: Quarterly Revenue Growth (year over year). Look for companies that are posting solid revenue growth.

- **Revenue (ttm)**: How much money they are bringing in compared to the group over the past trailing twelve months (ttm).

- **Gross Margin (ttm)**: How much they keep before paying bills over the past trailing twelve months.

- **EBITDA (ttm)**: Earnings Before Interest, Taxes, Depreciation and Amortization over the past trailing twelve months. How much they keep before all these are factored out. Pronounced as: e-b-tda

- **Operating Margin (ttm)**: It's one thing to make money; it's quite another how much of it the company is able to keep. Operating margins show how tight or generous a company's profits are after paying expenses over the past trailing twelve months.

- **Net Income (ttm)**: Net is just that – at the end of the period, just how much is banked over the past trailing twelve months. This is shown in the billions (B) and in the millions (M).

- **EPS (ttm)**: Earnings Per Share over the past trailing twelve months. Divide the profits by the number of shares issued. Yahoo Finance shows this as a dollar amount: 1.28 is: $1.28.

- **P/E (ttm)**: Price to Earnings Ratio over the past trailing twelve months. The price you would pay for a share of stock, based on a measurement using annual net earnings. A P/E of 19 means you would pay $19 for $1 of earnings. A high P/E of 50 is associated with a company that has a higher growth rate. A high P/E may not be relevant to your analysis when researching cloud computing companies.

- **PEG (5 yr expected)**: Price Earnings Growth is a company's expected P/E growth in the next five years.

- **P/S (ttm)**: Price-to-sales ratio over the past trailing twelve months. The math on this is similar to the P/E, except that the number of shares outstanding is divided by the annual sales instead of annual net earnings. Some on Wall Street like this indicator better than the P/E because you can't fudge sales numbers (they are what they are), while earnings are calculated after taxes, depreciation and a bunch of other accounting techniques.

REMEMBER: Any time you see a stock symbol in the color **blue**, it is a hyperlink. You can click on it, and the Internet will take you to the stock's profile page. As you continue viewing the Competitors page, it will show your company alongside both U.S. and non-U.S. companies "Ranked By Sales." This is a good time to click on those blue hyperlinks and check out the competition. You may just bump into more cloud computing companies to add to your cloud core list!

Now it's time to ask the second question to help build your cloud core list:

2) Does the company have a sustainable product or service advantage, and are they growing their bottom line profits?

You don't have to be an expert to know that you are looking for positive percentages that have been increasing over the past twelve months, and that continue to do so year over year.

Keep in mind that big-dog cloud companies are effective moneymakers. They have strong consumer appeal and a brand that can reinforce itself. That means they are moving forward and showing improvement in their financials, both in their products and services. You just have to know where to look.

Yahoo Finance – COMPANY > Key Statistics

On Wall Street, what's expected is a return on your investment. Return on assets and equity is just that: the percentage received back from money spent to run the business, invested capital. The question now becomes: is your cloud computing company profitable and moving forward?

Under the **COMPANY** list, scroll down and click on [**Key Statistics**] *(Exhibit No. 1, D:2)*. You are looking at two areas from **Financial Highlights** — **Management Effectiveness and Income Statement**.

Management Effectiveness

✓   Return on Assets

✓   Return on Equity

Income Statement

✓   Quarterly Revenue Growth

✓   Quarterly Earnings Growth

<u>**Management Effectiveness**</u>

Return on Assets (ttm)*	xx.xx%
Return on Equity (ttm)	xx.xx%

<u>**Income Statement**</u>

Revenue (ttm):	
Revenue Per Share (ttm):	
Qtrly Revenue Growth (yoy)**	xx.xx%
Gross Profit (ttm):	
EBITDA (ttm):	
Net Income Avl to Common (ttm):	
Diluted EPS (ttm):	
Qtrly Earnings Growth (yoy):	xx.xx%

* ttm = Trailing Twelve Months
** yoy = Year Over Year
   Qtrly = Quarterly

These quarterly growth percentages from the income statement are going to help you determine whether your cloud company is showing that steady growth pattern you'd expect to see from a big-dog cloud company with staying power.

Yahoo Finance — FINANCIALS > Balance Sheet

The next area to look at is a company's balance sheet. You want to know how they manage their cash and specifically their debt. Under **FINANCIALS,** click on [**Balance Sheet**] *(Exhibit No. 1, G:2)*. This section will help you size up their overall debt.

Growth and Debt

If a company has an enormous amount of debt, the concern is that they may not be able to post a profit, which would keep their stock price down. If a company is showing that they are reducing their debt quarter by quarter and year over year, this may indicate a brighter outlook. Don't get overly concerned if your cloud company is way in debt. Many of them are still developing and getting up to speed. Just keep an eye on their balance sheet to see if there is improvement over time.

Some cloud companies have been paying cash along the way and are debt free or have very little debt. In my cloud research, I was able to locate one cloud computing company that was debt free. At first I thought it was a mistake, a typo. I checked it out, and to my surprise, they were sitting on zero debt and a nice amount of free cash flow. I was impressed.

Yahoo Finance — FINANCIALS > Cash Flow

Scroll all the way down to the very bottom of the left tab to **FINANCIALS**, and click on [**Cash Flow**]. *(Exhibit No. 1, G:3)*. Now change the view from "**Annual Data**" to "**Quarterly Data**." (This is at the top of the page just under [**Cash Flow**].) What you want is at the top of this page: **Period Ending – Net Income**. This is going to show you how the company has done.

You have a choice to "**View**" this information as **Annual Data** or **Quarterly Data**. Since you're new at this, I suggest looking at both views.

As you review this information, ask yourself:

- Is the annual and quarterly net income increasing?
- Is a negative number getting smaller?
- Is a positive number getting larger?

In a perfect world, you want these numbers to improve. You and I both know stuff happens. Sometimes a company experiences a setback because of slower than expected orders or a strike could impact their bottom line. They may be using their free cash to buy company stock, which could reflect in their bottom line numbers. Their manufacturing facility could have been hurt by a power outage, which resulted in a plant slowdown or worse, a closure, which would affect their bottom line growth. So how would you know any of this? The news, of course!

Yahoo Finance — NEWS + INFO > Headlines

If you see a gap or drop in income you can't explain, check the news. **Yahoo Finance – NEWS & INFO** has a tab on the stock profile page for [**Headlines**] *(Exhibit No. 1, C:1)*. You're looking to see if they have announced earnings warnings and why. Was there a setback in net income as a result of Mother Nature or economic forces like a recession? You need know if they are starting to fall behind to new competition, or if it's just a hiccup.

Kick the Tires — Fundamental Analysis

This line of questioning has a couple of financial terms linked to it: **fundamental analysis,** also known as **bottom-up investing**. It looks for the competitive advantages of a company. This approach assumes that the company is the focus of your investigation. You don't place emphasis on the sector or any economic or market events taking place. This is a hands-on approach where you tear into the company, starting at the bottom, and pull it apart from the inside out. Think of this approach as kicking the tires of a car you want to buy, and then lifting up the hood to check out the engine.

Finding cloud computing companies is part science and part art, which is why some investors leave this up to the professionals. For those of you who are doing this on your own and have been successful, I tip my hat to you!

Keep in mind Wall Street analysts don't have a crystal ball. Neither do I and neither do you. We have tools and opinions. You, the investor, can check out the research and what analysts have to say, but at the end of the day, it comes down to you and your financial advisor — not the analysts — to make the final decision as to what is best for your portfolio. *You must do your own thinking and research.* Don't let Wall Street make you nervous or intimidate you. They are not the final authority!

Summary

1. Review the gap in price between the **Last Trade** and the **1y Target Est**. *(Exhibit No.1)*

2. See what Wall Street is saying about your company. **ANALYST COVERAGE [Analyst Opinion]** *(Exhibit No. 1, E:1)*
    Review these four sections:
    - Recommendation Summary
    - Price Target Summary
    - Upgrades and Downgrades History
    - Recommendation Trends

3. Order research reports to learn more about the company, and review the analyst projection on how it's expected to do going forward. **ANALYST COVERAGE [Research Reports]** *(Exhibit No. 1, E)*

4. Compare them to their competitors to see who they go head-to-head with. **COMPANY [Competitors]** *(Exhibit No. 1, D:3)*

5. Find out how effective management is in growing the business by comparing their return on assets and equity, their quarterly revenue, and earnings growth year over year. **COMPANY [Key Statistics]** *(Exhibit No.1, D:2)*

6. Find out if the company is posting profits and/or showing improvements on their balance sheet over the last quarter and over the last year. **FINANCIALS [Balance Sheet]** *(Exhibit No.1, G:2)*

7. Double check the cash flow. Ideally, your company should be increasing income, reducing debt and posting larger positive numbers. **FINANCIALS [Cash Flow]** *(Exhibit No.1, G:3)*

8. In Yahoo Finance or on a Google search, check headlines, company events, and blog posts to see what's been recently published about the company. You don't want to be surprised after the fact. **NEWS & INFO [Headlines]** *(Exhibit No. 1, C:1)*

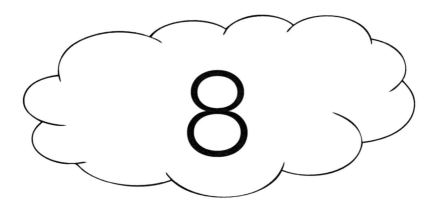

CIRRUS CLOUDS

LIFTING THE VEIL

"We are not trying to entertain the critics. I'll take my chances with the public."

WALT DISNEY

The Second Key Cloud Element — Cirrus Clouds

The more you know about clouds the better, and the best way to find out information about them is to use **search engines** and **web browsers.** Brace for liftoff — you are about to get hit with a wave of information, starting at **YouTube.**

YouTube

There are a few of you reading this thinking, "What is that?" YouTube is a virtual place on the Internet where you can find and watch videos. Companies and regular folks like you and me take their own digital movies, upload them on the site, and share them with the world. It's free and open to the public.

Once you are on the Internet, type their web address directly into your browser: www.youtube.com, and you're good to go. In the YouTube search box type: [**cloud computing**]. Now, sit back and take it all in.

On January 6, 2011, I ran this search and it resulted in 5,390 YouTube videos on cloud computing. Ninety days later I did this search again to see how many new YouTube videos were out there. On April 9, 2011, this same search landed me 17,300 cloud computing videos! I was amazed and then again, I wasn't. I realized early on that this was not just a fad but how we will all be doing business and living our lives sooner rather than later. It won't surprise me if when you do this search, the number will have grown even larger. Take some time to watch a few of these videos. Add the obvious ones to your core cloud list.

Here are subgroups that will come up on YouTube when you search "cloud computing." Randomly click on a few in each category and see what's going on.

- Cloud computing explained
- Cloud computing demo
- Cloud computing in plain English
- Cloud computing security

- Cloud computing funny
- Cloud computing applications
- Cloud computing Microsoft
- Cloud computing Google
- Cloud computing technology

Some of the videos that you'll see are produced by "big cloud" companies and are ads to sell a product. Some are educational. They want to show you how their stuff fits into your life. It's entertaining and you'll pick up a lot of info very quickly. As you watch these videos, keep in mind that all of these companies are calling out for your attention and your dollars.

Trade Shows

If you have some vacation time coming, check in to a technology or electronics trade show. The Consumer Electronics Show (CES) held in Las Vegas every January is literally a walk into the clouds. The best part of an electronics and technology expo is that you get to see prototypes of ideas that are still on the drawing board. Many items are launching right away or will be within a few months. You get first crack at what cloud companies are up to and you get to meet the newcomers to keep an eye on for later. You have the ability to ask questions and watch demonstrations.

I came home from the CES with several new ideas that would have taken me months to come across if I had not had the opportunity to attend. I love having a heads up before the crowd gets into a stock.

At trade shows and expos, you also get to see who companies are partnering with and all of the businesses that support this industry – all under one very large roof.

Still at the **YouTube** site, in the search box type in [**CES 2012**] (or any year you're interested in seeing).

- Check out what companies are saying about their lineup of new products or services.

- See which companies are doing the majority of posting.

- Get a preview of cutting-edge technology.

- Take time to scroll down the list of cloud computing companies and make notes on who's doing what…and if they mention who their *partners* are in projects. You want to pay close attention when a comment or mention is made of how something is made, and what other company products go into the final production of their item.

Add these key companies to your core cloud list.

High-Tech Beer Drinking!

My husband's (and one of my) favorite booth at the 2011 CES was the beer keg gone high-tech! It's posted on YouTube, if you want to see something fun and wacky. Look for "CES 2011 Kegputer."

Search Engines

The most common searches are done through search engines. **Internet search engines** are websites that have a search capability to find online data and deliver it to you. There are search engines designed for specific things like medical questions, legal issues, and finding work. You are going searching for clouds using search engines that provide data on "General," "Business," and "News."

Whichever search engine(s) you decide to use, you want to start your process by typing in the search box [**Cloud Computing**].

General Search Engines

- Ask.com (known as Ask Jeeves in the U.K.)

- Baidu (Chinese, Japanese)

- Bing (formerly MSN Search and Live Search)

- Blekko
- Duck Duck Go
- Google
- Sogou (Chinese)
- Soso (Chinese)
- Kosmix
- Yahoo
- Yandex (Russian)
- Yebol
- Yodao (Chinese) [1]

Business Search Engines

- Business.com
- GlobalSpec
- Nexis (Lexis Nexis)
- Thomasnet (United States)
- GenieKnows (United States and Canada) [2]

News Search Engines

- Bing News
- Google News
- Daylife
- MagPortal
- Newslookup
- Nexis (Lexis Nexis)
- Tropix

- Yahoo News [3]

From here, you can drill this down to more specific searches. I did a Yahoo search for the heck of it and typed in "Top cloud computing companies." My search came back with almost three million search results! Two million nine hundred thirty thousand, to be exact. Before you throw up your hands and quit — wait. This is really good. Those two million nine hundred thousand web pages are giving you info on a relatively small number of cloud companies. The best part is that all this information is public and available to everyone, from Wall Street to your kitchen table.

Additional Searches

- Data Centers — storage services
- Digital Analytics
- Broadband
- Broadcast and Cable
- Entertainment
  - Gaming
  - Personalized Apps
  - Internet Video
  - Video Platforms
- Home Area Networks (HAN)
- Internet Security
- Mobile Applications
  - Mobile Cloud Media
  - Apps
- Social Media
- VoIP (Voice Over Internet Protocol)
- Battery Backup

- Metal Case
- Cloud Fashions
- Mobile Providers for Cloud Computing
- 3-D Technology
- Internet TV Providers
- High-Tech Glass for Tablets
- Accessories
  - iPhone
  - iPad
  - Readers
  - Tablets
- Virtual Home
  - Appliances
  - Electrical
  - Security
  - Heating and Air
  - Remote Home Access
- Virtual Car
  - Audio
  - Accessories
  - Maps
  - Diagnosis
  - Teen Control Settings
  - Speed Control Settings
  - Electrical
  - Hybrid

- Health and Wellness
    - Home Health Care
    - Hearing or Sight-Impaired Enhancement Technology
    - Medical Tracking and Billing Software
    - Virtual Workouts
    - Fitness Games
- Digital Imaging and Photography
- Telecommunications Infrastructure
- Video
- Wireless
    - Devices
    - Embedded Technology
    - Tablets
    - Netbooks
    - WiFi [4]

Whew, and the list goes on.

Street Talk

A good portion of Wall Street is made up of "old guys" — the fifty-and-older group who are still licking their wounded egos after the dot-com bubble burst. Some have even turned against tech. Then you have the just-out-of-college group who got their first job as a junior analyst. They have no idea how the "old guys" could be so far out of the tech loop. These young analysts grew up plugged into the Internet. It's all they know. The only thing they are lacking is experience.

This clash of old and young is actually to your advantage. I suggest you follow a number of older analysts and some of the younger ones too. This will give you a good mix and balance for tracking stocks you all follow. The easiest way to do this is to set up a Google Alert, which will help you search out not only analysts, but also bloggers, newsletters, magazines and e-zines that can be valuable resources to find cloud computing companies.

Bloggers

A tech blogger is a person who writes about technology on a website. You don't need a subscription to read their blogs. They are there for you to access — just like my financial blog, www.BrillianceByBlonskij.com.

Blogging is not my full-time job, but for many, this is what they do. It's their passion. They eat and sleep blogging. These men and women are here for you 24/7, 365 days a year. They report on everything tech — tech tabloids! These blog sites give you information as it happens.

Bloggers are an uncensored group. They say whatever is on their mind and share with their readers many insights. Some bloggers are "rough around the edges" and their language can be crude. They make their point known in very few words. Like it or hate it, these guys and gals tell it like it is.

Bloggers cover every aspect of tech. Search for "cloud blogs," or be more specific and search "tablet PC bloggers," and a list of folks will come up. I have found bloggers to be a source of fresh data and new ideas. Find a few you like and subscribe to their RSS (Really Simple Syndication) feed. It's a free service. After you have read their posts for a few weeks, decide if you agree with their thinking or not. If they are adding value to your overall insights and investing plan — great! If not, stop the feed. If they like a cloud company, consider adding it to your list. You can always check it out and then take it off later if you don't like it.

Newsletters

There are financial and tech **newsletters** galore. Some will offer you a little bit of free information to see if you're interested in a subscription. They go to great lengths to point out what you should and should not buy. A number of newsletters that I've come across are very good. Others…well, you'll just have to see for yourself. Above all, don't rely on a newsletter or blogger to direct your decisions. They are there to offer insights, opinions, and ideas to help you in your research. If you find a newsletter you like and it's in your budget, you may want to consider a subscription. It could turn out to be a good investment in the long run. Start with the minimum they offer. If you like it, you can always renew.

An online newsletter I've used is produced by The Motley Fool. They offer a lot of different types of research and information. They are not beholden to anyone, any company, or any brokers, which means they can say whatever they darn well want to and not worry about stepping on toes. From time to time, they may try to sell you a book or seminar package, which is okay by me. After all, they have to make money too. They produce videos and have Fool gatherings around the country that you can attend to meet other Motley Fool followers. Their website is www.fool.com.

Please remember, investing is *NOT* "one-size-fits-all." If you do decide to buy a subscription to a newsletter on investing, keep in mind you're unique and the company or organization producing the newsletter may be selling a cookie-cutter investment idea that is not tailored to you. Use it as a tool, not a crutch.

Magazines

Old-fashioned print magazines are among the oldest research tools. There are so many to choose from, depending on what you're interested in. Pick up a paper copy at the corner store, or download one online.

E-Zines

The new term you may hear for a magazine publication you get off the Internet is **e-zine,** which is short for "<u>e</u>lectronic maga<u>zine</u>." Below is a partial list of e-zines I pulled off of the site world-newspapers.com. Some of these I have read cover to cover; others I just glance through to see what catches my eye or for something that's out of the ordinary.

- **CNET News:** Breaking news, features and special reports covering tech and its impact on e-business, finance, communications, personal technology and entertainment. http://news.cnet.com/

- **IEEE Spectrum Magazine:** Explores future technology trends and the impact of those trends on society and business. http://spectrum.ieee.org/

- **InfoWorld:** Tech magazine for IT news, products, reviews, best practices and white papers covering security, storage, virtualization, open source and more. http://www.infoworld.com/

- **Investors.com (eIBD):** The parent company of eIBD, Investors Business Daily, was started by a couple of stockbrokers back in the late 1950's. Today, it's very diverse offering stock research, news and editorials, education, a community forum and group meet-ups. http://www.investors.com

- **Mobile Magazine:** Covers news and reviews on mobile technology, including cell phones, PDAs, MP3 players and digital cameras. http://www.mobilemag.com/

- **Red Herring Magazine:** Providing news and information for the research and development community. http://www.redherring.com/

- **PC World:** Popular computer magazine offering advice on different aspects of PC and related items. They feature the Top 100 PC and product rankings, evaluations, ratings, tips, how-to's, step-by-step guides and more. http://www.pcworld.com/#new

- **PC Magazine:** A complete guide to all things PC, from computers to upgrades. They review computer and Internet-related products, report on technology news and trends, and provide shopping advice and price comparisons. http://www.pcmag.com/

- **Wired:** In-depth coverage of current and future trends in technology and how they are shaping business, entertainment, communications, science, politics and culture. http://www.wired.com/ [5]

For a longer list of technology magazines and news sites, go to:

www.world-newspapers.com
www.world-newspapers.com/technology.html
www.world-newspapers.com/computer.html

NOTE: Check out the "editor's favorites" section in each edition. You just may find some good pieces of information packed in his or her comments. After all, editors get to see everything from twenty thousand feet above ground level on a monthly basis.

STRATUS CLOUDS

OUT IN THE OPEN

"We allow no geniuses around our studio."

WALT DISNEY

The Third Key Cloud Element — Stratus Clouds

Up till now you have been compiling a lot of cloud ideas from a number of sources to make up your list of possible companies to own. Now you are going to take a different approach. You are going to find the cloud companies you missed that are still under the radar! I'm talking about those companies that help make the "big clouds" look good. The ones that make it possible for our devices to work and our apps to run on demand. You are going to step back and follow the technology to its roots by doing what's called **reverse engineering.**

Yahoo Finance — COMPANY > Profile (Investor Relations)

Start with a "big cloud" company you've identified by heading over to their company website. An easy way to get this link is through Yahoo Finance. Under **COMPANY**, click on [**Profile**] *(Exhibit No.1, D:1).* The company's address and website will be at the top of the page. The website will be a blue hyperlink so you can click on it and the hyperlink will take you right to their home page.

You'll want to locate the **Investor Relations** tab on the home page. This is usually found at the top right corner of the website, but it can also be at the very bottom on the home page. If the company is publicly traded, the tab will be there; keep looking until you find it.

Once you are on the Investor Relations page, click on **Annual Report.** The most recent year will do. You are looking for **"licensing agreements"** in the table of contents. Licensing agreements tell "the rest of the story" on who is doing what in relationships with your cloud company. It's like asking an auto company who they use as a supplier for the leather interior, the nice plastic-looking wood and the car stereo. How about the motor, belts and spark plugs? If auto makers laid out every one of their vendors, that would be your road map to see who else profits from car sales.

As you are reverse-engineering, keep an eye out for:

- Partnerships
- Licensing Agreements
- Joint Ventures
- Distributors
- Manufacturing Facilities

The second part to this would be all those other businesses that support your car after you've driven it home — the auto parts house, your oil and lube stores, windshield repair places, and paint and body shops. For every car sold there is a larger network of services and providers that support the safety and comfort of your car. This same principle holds true for cloud computing companies. Cloud companies are the same as the auto industry in this context, except it's a virtual experience.

Ask yourself:

- What additional items are needed to run the business?
- Who and where are supplies coming from?
- How is it delivered?
- Who are the company's top clients?
- Where else do their clients order and buy from?

Yahoo Finance — COMPANY > Competitors

Go back to **Yahoo Finance** and get a list of their [**Competitors**] *(Exhibit No. 1, D:3)*. Evaluate them in the same way and you will begin to see who the main players are in the industry — those who support your cloud companies and their competitors. Reverse engineering is a good way to follow the technology and the money back to their roots. Once you know who manufactures for them and where they get product support from, you will be at the next level.

Where you could get stuck is if they do it all in house. In that case, there is no reverse engineering to be done. If you are researching devices, you will find suppliers both in production and in after-sale support. If you are researching software like apps providers, there may not be a long trail to follow.

I pulled up the 2009 annual report for a well-known coffee house just to prove my point. I wanted to see who was supplying their additional products. To my delight and surprise, I found out a bunch of stuff I took for granted and all from their annual report.

For example, the company licenses the right to produce and market branded products with several partnerships both domestically and internationally. In the annual report, they name their partners. One is a well-known soft drink company. I discovered a U.S. food service company that works with them to channel their products into restaurants, airports, hospitals, and more places. They use six dairies between the U.S. and Canada. I got all this from spending less than seven minutes pulling up their annual report.

Yahoo Finance — OWNERSHIP> Insider Transactions

This is the inside scoop! This area of your research deals with company stock and stock options that are exercised (bought and sold) by company insiders like directors and executives. **Insider Transactions** is "public" information. It's allowed to use in your research and easy to find.

As part of a disclosure rule, officers and directors of companies that are publicly traded have to report their trade information to the U.S. Securities and Exchange Commission (SEC) every time they buy, sell, or exercise a stock option on their company's stock. This data is reviewed, published, and available to the public online. It's the "inside scoop" I'm talking about. Here is why you want to check this out:

Let's say you are the president of a cloud computing company that is doing great. The company is on fire and is eating the competition's lunch day in and day out. You are given company stock as part of your salary — it's an incentive to keep the company profitable, and you are doing a super job. Everyone loves you. Your staff, the board of directors, stockholders, your wife and kids — everyone! The company stock is breaking 52-week highs every month since you've taken over. Then one day, out of the blue, you sell 100 percent of every stock and stock option you own. What just happened? What is wrong with this picture? The law states, that as president of the company, you have to disclose to the world that you just sold all your stock. Take the same example and say you are that same president, except this time you decide that with your million-dollar end-of-the-year bonus, you are going to purchase company stock. This too has to be reported and made public.

You, the reader, have access to this kind of information at your fingertips. As investors we can't trade on non-public information, but if it's public, we can use it to help make decisions.

Here's how to get the inside scoop with insider transactions. In **Yahoo Finance**, scroll down and on the left side under **OWNERSHIP**, click on **[Insider Transactions]** (*Exhibit No.1, F:2*). This is going to show you how many shares were transacted by "insiders." Directors and officers are listed by name, and by how many shares they bought or sold and the date. As my dad used to say, "Actions speak louder than words."

Company Buy-Back

The last inside scoop is to find out what the company is doing with their money. When a company board of directors approves buying back some of their company stock, it's announced in the press. Just like you, they have to buy it in the open market on the stock exchange.

If your cloud company is buying back stock, a couple of questions come to mind right away. Does their board of directors recognize a good value in their own company? Have they decided to buy some of their stock back as an investment? Or – are they trying to add volume to their stock to keep it from going lower?

Check blog posts and the news to get a feel for which of the two is happening. It will help you decide if it's time for you to buy or time to move on.

NOTE: Insider information is "private" information and against the law to use. Private company information that has not been released to the public is not legal to trade. If, in a casual conversation or in overhearing someone in a conversation, you pick up on news about a publicly traded company that is not in the public realm and you act on it, or you give the information to someone else to act on, you will have broken the law and will suffer financial penalties and possible jail time.

The Outside Scoop

The outside scoop is just that — information about the company from sources not directly involved with the business. And there are a slew of outside sources.

Financial TV

Here on the West Coast, I wake up with a strong cup of coffee and tune in to **CNBC's "Squawk on the Street."** They make starting my day fun as I get ready for work. Before I'm out the door, I know what's going on in Asia, Europe, what the bond market is doing, where oil and currencies are and how the U.S. market looks to open. I'm all set and ready to roll, and you should be too. Another favorite of mine is "**Mad Money**" on **CNBC**. This is a fun-packed show, chock-full of information that will educate and entertain you all at the same time. If you don't have cable TV, the **Nightly Business Report** on **PBS** (Public Broadcasting Service) is an excellent recap of the day's events.

Digital video recorders (DVRs) allow you to record and watch these shows anytime, at your convenience. With wireless devices you can even take financial TV with you. Technology can deliver them to your cloud computing devices. If an analyst makes a comment on one of these shows and it gets posted on the network website, BOOM! In comes a news story to your computer or cell phone. All you have to do is open it up.

Education and Dedication

Next, find several **economists, analysts, and journalists** to follow. They should not all be in agreement with each other — or with you, for that matter. Here are some I follow and why.

Steve Forbes, president and CEO of Forbes and Forbes Magazine, in which he shares commentary on business, taxes, investments, you name it. I got to see him in person at an event in Sacramento years ago. I was so impressed, I've paid attention to him ever since.

Joseph Meyer is a 40-year veteran of the securities industry and worked with the NASD (National Association of Security Dealers). I first heard him on "Coast to Coast," a late-night talk radio show, and found his comments compelling. He writes a monthly newsletter, *Straight Money Analysis*, that's easy to read. I want to know what Mr. Meyer has to say and I value his knowledge and experience.

Charles Nenner. He predicts the market based on cycles, and has developed tools for just about everything from stocks to gold to oil.

Nouriel Roubini, professor of economics at New York University. Roubini is a former senior economist for President Bill Clinton and worked at the Federal Reserve and World Bank. He knows money on a global level better than most.

Rick Sherlund, is a veteran analyst starting out at Goldman Sachs back in 1982. In March of 2011, he joined Nomura Securities as their Director of Technology Research. He has been recognition by his peers as a "top-ranked" tech analyst. In my opinion, Rick is one of the most responsible voices in technology today.

Liz Ann Sonders, senior vice president and chief investment strategist at Charles Schwab. I find her work to be a calm voice of reason when it's cloudy in the markets. Liz Ann is optimistically cautious. I like her style. Her research is well-presented and is available online to customers and non-customers at no cost.

Byron Wien and I both worked for the same Wall Street firm many years ago. Byron was our senior investment strategist. He is still around and I keep tabs on what he has to say.

Straight Talk

Start a conversation with the experts in their individual fields. When you read an article that connects with you, send the author an e-mail. This can open up a channel of communication. You may be surprised by just how receptive many of these writers are. They are happy to get your feedback and comments. I've done it several times and made some good connections along the way.

Public Plans

Keep an eye on public **pension plans** by setting up a Google Alert on their news releases. I got wind of a European money manager, who runs a highly specialized investment, just by tapping into my state's press releases. From that one news story, I was able to do some reverse engineering. I found a couple of new investment ideas that I could have overlooked had it not been for this alert.

Summary

You just never know where your next inspiration is coming from. There are many ways to get the inside and outside scoops! I'm sure you can think of even more ways to dig up information that will help you own cloud computing companies.

1. Review and evaluate management, new services, product improvements and competitive pricing. **COMPANY** [**Profile**] (*Exhibit No. 1, D:1*)

2. Use the blue hyperlink under **COMPANY** [**Profile**] to click on the company web site. You are looking for the tab on their home page listed as "**Investor Relations**" to pull up their annual report, and locate their business partners. Keep an eye out for:

   • Partnerships

   • Licensing Agreements

- Joint Ventures
- Distributors
- Manufacturing Facilities

3. Pull up a list of their major competition to get more insight on how well they do going head to head. Look for additional cloud-related companies to consider investing into. **COMPANY [Competitors]** *(Exhibit No.1, D:3)*

4. Now get the inside scoop on what management is doing with their stock holdings. **OWNERSHIP [Insider Transactions]** *(Exhibit No.1, F:2)*

5. Tune into blog posts and financial TV. **Yahoo Finance — NEWS & INFO [Financial Blogs]** *(Exhibit No. 1, C:2)*

6. Follow several economists and journalists.

7. Start conversations. Send out comments when you read or see a post that grabs your interest.

8. Key an eye on public pension plans to get ideas on what they are doing with their investments.

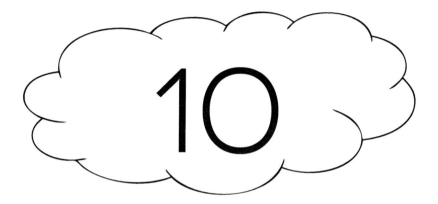

CUMULUS CLOUDS
CHARTING THE CLOUDS

"Of all of our inventions for mass communication, pictures still speak the most universally understood language."

WALT DISNEY

The Fourth Key Cloud Element — Cumulus Clouds

Would you build a home without a hammer? Of course not! Would you own a restaurant without a stove to cook on? Well, maybe – more than likely, you would have some other way to prepare food. Charting the clouds is the fourth key cloud element. Charts can help you make investment decisions. Charts are a tool of the trade. If you are investing in the stock market, you'll want to use them.

Charts offer investors another vantage point. It's like looking down at your city from an airplane; all of a sudden, there is a break in the sky, and your city is in clear view. You get a totally different perspective of where you live and work. Charting your path is critical, and a stock chart is a valuable tool.

Charts are not going to argue or debate with you. They are a non-emotional gauge. They stand on their own merit. As you learn what to look for, you'll start to recognize different patterns. These patterns will give you additional guidance and can confirm or dispel your feelings to buy or sell a company. A stock chart is used to help you spot changes in strength, direction, momentum and duration of a stock price trend.

If you are hoping I am going to give you an advanced lesson on charting, sorry – I won't be getting that deep into charts. However, I will show you how to identify some of the signals charts display and to spot a trend a stock may be forming.

The charts we will be looking at are developed and plotted using past price performance. These price changes are calculated and then put into charts and histograms (bar graphs) using a process called autocorrelation.

AUTOCORRELATION

Some of you reading this are thinking, *This is getting complicated.* Let me break this down into easy sound bytes, and then explain why you want to know about this when looking at charts.

AUTOCORRELATION

- "AUTO" refers to a **process**.
- "COR" means **together**.
- "RELATION" is a **common** tie.

An example of autocorrelation would be writing down your daily weight on a calendar every morning for a year. Now, take your daily weight from all those mornings and plot them. You'd probably start by running a 365 daily chart. You may want to run it again, showing your weight every Monday morning by running a 52-week chart. You can take the same information and run a chart showing the last 90 days, or whatever you'd like.

Now, overlay each of the charts on the same graph. You should be able to see a weight loss trend over different time periods.

- If you stay within a couple of pounds, the trend line will be pretty flat.
- If you're gaining weight, the trend line will point upward.
- If you're losing weight, the trend line will point downward.

When applied to the stock market, autocorrelation uses price points (typically the closing price of the day) on an individual stock over a series of time periods. The days used to collect this information are called **data points**, and the process to sort and chart them is called **time series analysis**.

Looking Back — Time Series Analysis

Time series analysis gathers and compiles information that will eventually be used to plot a graph. It looks at what the stock did in the past. Once the chart is done, it's now up to you to decide the future direction.

Think of this as if you were taking your blood pressure over a 30-day period. Each day would be a "data point," and the 30 days would be your "time series." You can easily plot this on a graph. If your blood pressure has been going up, the chart will have an upward bias. However, that does not mean that for the next 30 days you will have the same average blood pressure, or that it will continue to go higher and higher! You're looking back at what it was and not necessarily what it will be.

Time series analysis shows you where the stock price has been. It is not, however, the final test of a stock before you hit the [**Enter**] button on your computer to "buy" or "sell." Charts are used to help you recognize where a stock has come from, and possibly, the direction it may be headed.

Four Data Components

Just like taking your blood pressure every day for a month, "things" can change that affect you and your blood pressure. As in life, "things" can get in the way of your stock price.

There are four areas investors need to be aware of when looking at data that can get in the way and possibly change the direction of a stock they're following. As you review a stock chart, keep in mind these four data components:

1. Trends

2. Cycles

3. Seasonality

4. Surprises

Trends

A stock price trend can be easy to recognize, especially if the trend has been going on for some time and the direction has been established. If the stock price has an upward bias, the chart will show an upward trend line. If the price has been going lower, then the trend line will be pointing downward.

Dates = "Time Series"

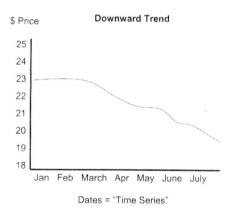

Dates = "Time Series"

There will be times when the direction of the trend line is harder to pinpoint. You may not see a strong movement in either direction. The stock may be moving sideways. When this occurs, you will need to do some additional research before making an investment decision.

Cycles

These are the price cycles, or waves, in stock price movements that are predictable over time.

One of my favorite examples of a cycle is a person who is overeating and sitting around all day. Before she knows it, she's gained 10 unwanted pounds. When her jeans won't zip, the alarms start going off in her head, and the next day she's on a strict diet. After some time passes, the 10 pounds are gone. She's back into her jeans, but there is just one problem. This type of person is a yo-yo dieter. Before she knows it, BOOM. Those 10 pounds are back and the cycle of dieting starts all over again. Yo-yo dieting is a cycle of predictable movements over time.

In your investing life, you'll find companies that cycle — which can make for a good opportunity to buy low and wait for the stock to cycle up to take a profit. Park the proceeds and then you can wait for the stock to cycle down and buy it back again.

I bought and sold IBM stock a number of years back using their price cycles to pop in and out of the stock. The stock would trade between $90 and $105 a share. It repeated this cycle for years before it made new highs.

Seasonality

This refers to the aspect of the time of year in which a stock price may normally move higher or lower. Take, for example, a toy company. Typically, their stock price should move higher during the Christmas season when toy sales are at their best, and lower into the summer months. Straw hat sales tend to be more robust in the summer, and umbrella sales do better in the winter. Some companies you follow will have a seasonality trait you'll need to be aware of when reviewing their stock chart.

Surprises

These are those completely out-of-the-blue, unexpected, random, and unpredictable events that can either make a stock value explode to higher price limits or get clobbered. As an investor, you have no idea when or if a stock will get a surprise. The Boy Scouts have a saying that fits perfectly in the event of a stock surprise: Be prepared at all times. Later, I'll touch on "**stop orders**" that can help protect a stock that's dropping in value.

Strong Versus Weak Trends

As you compare charts, be aware that you will be reviewing a lot of the same data using different time periods. This can give you a false positive, especially if the basis for a trend is weak.

It is possible that a new trend (one that's just getting started) could break down and go the other direction. When we get into Bollinger Bands later on, you'll see that when a strong trend has been confirmed, it's not likely to change direction, provided there aren't any random surprises thrown into the mix.

When you review a stock chart that's been trending in one direction over a number of different time periods, you could make a case that the stock price may continue to match the past price trends and move accordingly.

Understanding Autocorrelation

Most of the stock charting tools that are available to you from the Internet use autocorrelation analysis. It's important, as an investor, to understand and recognize that for the most part, you're seeing the same data sorted in a number of different ways, all using some variation of closing prices over a past time period. When you are using price points for the primary basis of your charts, the resulting graphs will show **similarities.** To evaluate your stock from different angles of analysis, take a look at the daily range in volume and at the **Put/Call Ratios**.

Put/Call Ratios – Future Forecasting

Buying or selling "puts" and/or "calls" options is an investment strategy used to speculate on the future direction of a stock or a stock market index. These orders can be very short term (days and weeks), or out a couple of years.

It's well-known that the vast majority of "option" buyers are not the most successful! "On balance, options buyers lose about 90% of the time."[1]

When this group gets excited and heated up, the buying frenzy begins. Their overly optimistic feelings kick in (**market sentiment**), and as a result a higher number of "buy" orders are placed, pushing up the "call" side of the ratio. Just the opposite happens when this group is running for cover.

Knowing this group's bleak record of success, following the put/call ratio is a good **contrarian-sentiment indicator** that can be used to bet against the crowd. By tracking the daily and weekly number of options orders, you can gauge how these traders are feeling about the future of a stock or the market.

The Options Exchange

Options data is complied and available through the Chicago Board Options Exchange (CBOE) at www.cboe.com/. From the CBOE web site click and hold on the tab [**Quotes & Data**] and select **Inter-Day Volume** from the drop down menu. Or you can use this link, which will take you to the CBOE's website showing the number of options trades placed: http://www.cboe.com/data/IntraDayVol.aspx. Their website is packed with a lot of timely information, and they also offer free classes if you want to dig in and learn more.

Charting Services

Start by checking out free charting services. There are lots out there to choose from: Yahoo Finance, Google Finance or StockCharts.com, just to name a few. You can use charts from my website, http://www.blonskij.com, and from dozens or more online investment firms. You can also pay for advanced charting services. I use a paid service from *Wealth Magazine* called Investools.

Basic Line Chart

This first chart to know about is a basic line chart. I am going to use a chart on Cisco Systems, Inc. This is not a recommendation to buy or sell this stock. This is for illustrative purposes only. I've found it's easier to explain, and it's more likely you'll use the information, if you can relate it to something familiar.

A basic line chart has a few key parts to it.

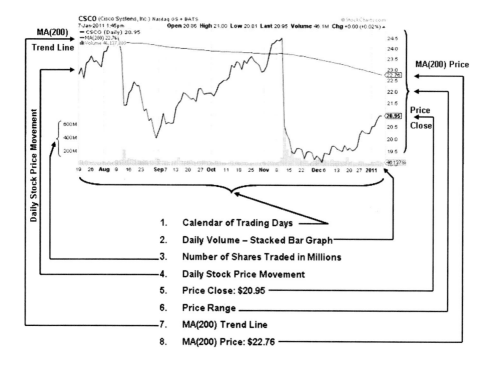

1.   Calendar of Trading Days
2.   Daily Volume – Stacked Bar Graph
3.   Number of Shares Traded in Millions
4.   Daily Stock Price Movement
5.   Price Close: $20.95
6.   Price Range
7.   MA(200) Trend Line
8.   MA(200) Price: $22.76

Chart courtesy of www.StockCharts.com

As an investor, you want to be familiar with how to read and understand the information provided in a basic chart. Here is a simple recap to explain the different sections shown in the Cisco chart above.

115

1. **Calendar of Trading Days:** Month and day, time line. Online charts allow you to change the view from a day view to months or even years. The calendar on the chart will adjust along with the chart view you choose. These days are "data points" used in autocorrelation.

A basic chart gives you a quick snapshot of how the stock and various indicators have performed over a period of time. The first chart you'll pull up on Yahoo Finance is a day chart and shows hours rather than days, months or years. To change your view, just click on the blue hyperlink below the chart that looks like this: 1d 5d 3m 6m 1y 2y 5y max *(Exhibit No.1, H).*

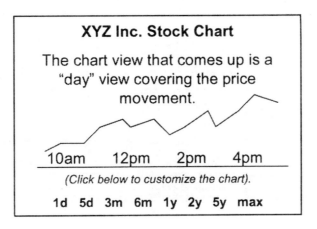

- 1d = that day's trading.
- 5d = the current and last four trading days.
- 3m, 6m = the last three or six months.
- 1y, 2y, or 5y = the last year, two years, or five years.
- max = since inception.

2. **Daily Volume – Stacked Bar Graph:** These columns (stacked bar graph also called a histogram) running horizontally along the bottom of the chart indicate how many shares actually traded on that given day. Volume can be light (meaning a few shares were traded) to heavy (indicating volatility in the stock).

3. **Number of Shares Traded in Millions:** This side bar is a gauge showing the number of shares traded from two hundred million up to six hundred million a day.

4. **Daily Stock Price Movement:** This jagged line (tend line) that moves up and down throughout the chart is the daily price movement per share.

5. **Price close: $20.95:** This is the closing price per share on the last business day shown on this chart (7-Jan-2011 1:45pm).

6. **Price Range:** The price range for this chart spans from $19.50 up to $24.50.

7. **MA(200) Trend Line:** The smooth line (trend line) running through the center of the chart is the moving average (MA). The two hundred (200) in parentheses is the number of days the stock price was averaged out over the time period in this chart. The moving average is figured by adding the closing stock price, of every day for the past two hundred days, and dividing it by the number of days (200). You end up with a smooth line that tracks the price.

8. **MA(200) Price: $22.76:** In the chart above, the moving average for the stock over the past two hundred days is $22.76. The MA (200) is using time series analysis.

Check out the stock charts at both Google Finance and Yahoo Finance. They offer a lot of the same data, but it's presented differently. I like both layouts.

Spotting Trends

Before you dig into a couple of my favorite charts, let's take a step back for just a moment and let me share with you a very difficult period in the market for technology stocks. Many cloud companies were putting their stakes in the ground in the mid 90s and experienced the dot-com bubble in 2002. Some have made it and survive today. Others didn't and are gone. A few are reinventing themselves or have found a niche and are doing amazing things with their cloud businesses. Some of the tech companies experienced a slow ten-year climb back to their 1999 highs. There are yet more companies that missed the comeback and are still trying to figure out how to compete in the clouds. Sadly, some of these companies may be left behind.

During a market event, like a dot-com bubble or a recession, stocks in general go lower. Don't let the dot-com part of your chart concern you too much. You will want to get concerned when the entire sector is going up and your chart shows your stock price as flat or dropping. This would be a big, flashing red cloud sign. There is a saying by market technicians: "Markets are efficient," which translates to the smart and strong will survive and thrive.

Emotional investing is often a gut reaction usually triggered by either fear or greed. Technical analysis boiled down to a basic concept takes actual stock data and puts it through a number of testing formulas that produce charts and histograms. Understanding a stock chart can tell you a lot; however, it is like driving and looking in the rearview mirror. You know where you were, but now you want to know where you or, in this case, your stock, is going. When you know what you're looking for on a chart it can help you determine a higher or lower price movement. Charts takes just a few minutes to read and move on — like our next chart on moving average convergence/divergence! It actually takes longer to say than to see what it's saying, once you know what to look for.

Moving Average Convergence/Divergence — MACD

It's time to layer in more charting tools. Next is the MACD (Moving Average Convergence/Divergence) chart. Pronounced as: mac-de. The MACD is one of the simplest charts to use and visually easy to understand. When you pull up the MACD you can immediately see the ebbs and flows in the chart on a day-by-day basis, which means you're in a better position to identify a trend.

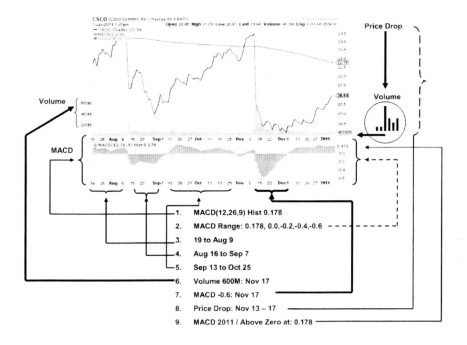

1. MACD(12,26,9) Hist 0.178
2. MACD Range: 0.178, 0.0,-0.2,-0.4,-0.6
3. 19 to Aug 9
4. Aug 16 to Sep 7
5. Sep 13 to Oct 25
6. Volume 600M: Nov 17
7. MACD -0.6: Nov 17
8. Price Drop: Nov 13 – 17
9. MACD 2011 / Above Zero at: 0.178

Chart courtesy of www.StockCharts.com

1. **MACD(12,26,9) Hist 0.178:** MACD is short for Moving Average Convergence/Divergence. This is a short-term indicator. When it's plotted on a graph, it looks like a depth finder and, in a way, that's what this is. This is a very straightforward indicator. The short time frames that are used make this indicator effective in spotting momentum and trends.

You just learned about a simple moving average (MA) on the basic line chart. The MACD uses three time periods: 12-day, 26-day, and a 9-day simple moving average. It starts by taking the 12- and 26-day simple moving average, and subtracts them to come up with one value. This value is then compared with an even shorter time line, a 9-day moving average. When the blended 12- and 26-day averages move above or below the 9-day average, it signals an overbought or oversold level which is what you are seeing, plotted on the MACD Histogram.

MACD Calculation:

- **MACD:** The 12-day EMA (Exponential Moving Average) is subtracted from the 26-day EMA, to come up with one value.

- **Signal Line:** This second moving average is calculated using a 9-day moving average, called the "**Signal Line**."

- **MACD Histogram:** MACD minus the Signal Line.

The MACD-Histogram represents the difference between the MACD and the 9-day EMA. The chart is positive when the MACD is above its 9-day EMA, and negative when the MACD is below its 9-day EMA.[2]

2. **MACD Range: 0.178, 0.0, -0.2,-0.4, -0.6:** The MACD moves from a negative to a positive number. It moves based on the moving averages we just looked at. Zero is the center line. When the MACD moves above and below zero, it's signaling a move in the stock price. In our sample chart, the low point for Cisco was -0.6 and the high point was at 0.179, which is the MACD Range for this chart.

3. **July 19 to Aug 9:** The start of a six-month period. During the period of July 19 to August 9, the MACD was above zero. The 12- and 26-day EMAs were above the 9-day EMA.

4. **Aug 16 to Sep 7:** The MACD is below zero. Notice the stock price has dropped and volume has increased.

5. **Sep 13 to Oct 25:** The MACD is above zero. The stock is moving up.

6. **Volume 600M: Nov 17:** On November 17 the volume on Cisco was tremendous. The scale on the side of the chart shows daily volume range from two hundred million shares up to six hundred million shares, and Cisco was trading up at the top range.

7. **MACD -0.6: Nov 17:** On November 17 the spike in trading volume took this indicator from a positive number (above zero) the day prior, to a negative number at the close of business that day.

8. **Price Drop: Nov 13-17:** With the spike in selling pressure (lack of buyers) that's reflected in nearly six hundred million shares trading, the stock price was push down from approximately $24 into the $19 range.

9. **MACD 2011/Above Zero at: 0.178:** In the Cisco chart the MACD is back above zero (lack of sellers) at a positive 0.178 – which is reflected in the higher price of the stock.

Bollinger Bands

One of my favorite charts is a **Bollinger Band**. Bollinger Bands have been around since the 1980s and were created by none other than a stock market fellow named John Bollinger. There are books devoted to explaining this charting tool, as well as tons of information you can get off the Internet. My plan in showing you how to use Bollinger Bands is to use the KISS principle: "keep it simple." You won't be a Bollinger Band expert but you will learn the beginnings of a very cool tool to use as you examine your stocks.

Bollinger Band charts help investors to confirm which direction a stock price may be moving. The upper and lower bands appear as lines on the stock charts that sandwich and follow the stock price's ups and downs. When they come together in a "squeeze," the magic happens — one way or the other!

Let me show you what I mean with the next two charts. They are nearly identical — *nearly* being the keyword. When I put these two charts together, I wanted to show you just how similar the bands behave in the bullish and bearish environments, as a stock price moves higher and lower. The two charts below use the same Bollinger Band outlines. The significant change is the stock price movement.

Bollinger Band Squeeze - Bullish

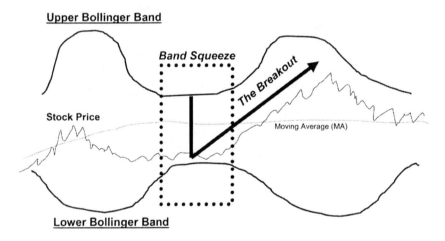

3 Components of Bollinger Bands:

1. **Upper Bollinger Band**

2. **Lower Bollinger Band**

3. **Middle Band** *This is a simple moving average (SMA)*

Band Squeeze

Bollinger Bands are best known and used for confirming "**The Squeeze.**" As the bands narrow and then widen the direction of the stock price changes, which can confirm a new developing trend. There are times when the direction is not confirmed and reverses the other way. However, a strong breakout will hold up.

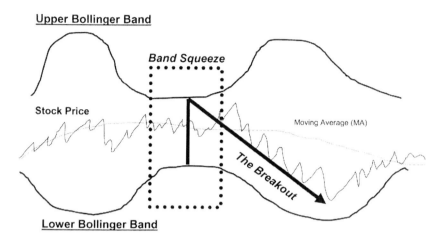

Bollinger Band Squeeze - Bearish

Narrow Band: A narrow band signals "**The Squeeze**." This is the result of heavy trading volume in the stock and, of course, several calculations running in the background of the chart.

Narrow Band = The Squeeze

Wide Band: The wider the band, the higher or lower the stock price will continue on its directional path. If you have ever gone fishing, it's like when you hook a big fish — you've set the hook, and the fish starts to "run." It's the same thing with wide bands. As the bands widen, the stock is on a run.

Wide Band = The Breakout

Bollinger Bands will normalize and come back into a channel. The stock price will stabilize and trade in a *normal* range (which may be a *new* normal for the stock), until another squeeze appears on the charts.

Bollinger Bands — Cisco Chart

Let's get a real-world look at Bollinger Bands using our same Cisco chart. Just after November, the volume skyrocketed to nearly six hundred million shares. This is not a typical day for the stock. Stock sales were dominant, meaning there were very few investors standing in line to purchase the stock. With the *increased volatility* (another way of saying heavy volume), the stock price dropped and the Bollinger Bands *widened*.

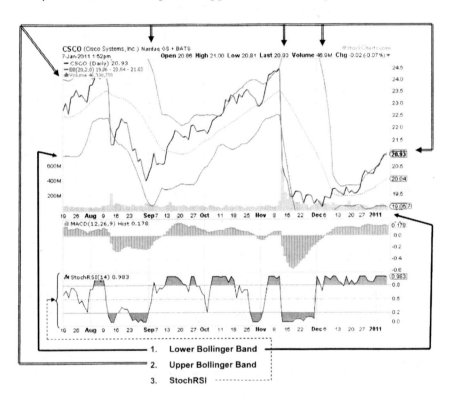

1. **Lower Bollinger Band**
2. **Upper Bollinger Band**
3. **StochRSI**

Chart courtesy of www.StockCharts.com

As the bands start to *tighten* (mid-December) and squeeze together, the stock price finds a footing and the volatility slows down; the bands move closer, and the price settles out. As the bands *widen* (early 2011), the stock price moves again, this time higher.

Bollinger Bands make me think of a snake eating a pig. The snake opens its mouth wide and the pig goes in. Then, it's on the move — as the pig is digested it travels through the body. When it's fully digested, the snake's body goes back to its normal size range.

When Bollinger Bands start to *widen*, the stock price is like the pig inside the snake — it's got to go someplace! So does the stock price. As the bands widen, the number of shares being bought or sold (the volume) adds pressure and moves the bands. No pressure and the bands move in a narrow range.

Both the lower and upper Bollinger Bands are a **directional guide**.

- **Increased Volatility = Bands Widen**
- **Decreased Volatility = Bands Narrow**

StochRSI – Stochastic Oscillator, Relative Strength Index (RSI)

The Stochastic Oscillator (Stoch) is another charting tool that **measures the price** of a stock in relation to the **high *and* low** range over a set period of time. This indicator signals when a stock is overbought (1.0) or oversold (0.0). Below 0.2 or 20 is considered extreme oversold, and above 0.8 or 80 is considered extreme overbought.

- 1.0 = Extremely Overbought

- 0.0 = Extremely Oversold

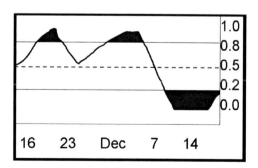

If you are a "day trader," this tool is going to come in handy, since day traders typically look for extremes to enter or exit a stock.

Yahoo Finance — CHARTS > Basic Tech Analysis

The MACD, Bollinger Bands, and StochRSI are three different types of charting tools that will help you identify a trend. The next time you are on **Yahoo Finance,** scroll down to **CHARTS** and click on [**Basic Tech Analysis.**] *(Exhibit No.1, B)* From this charting page you can go wild. It's like being a kid in a candy store! You'll realize quickly just how many different types of charting tools are there waiting for you to discover.

The Last Word on Charts

- Charts will slow you down when you're afraid and want to sell.

- Charts will slow you down when your excitement out weights your common sense.

- Charts help you know when it is time to move on, hold on, or buy more.

- Charts help you identify a trend. You'll know when it's time to just sit back and let a stock run and not get out too early — or ever, in some cases.

- Charts let you see where the stock is on a 200-day or a 10-day moving average (MA).

- Charts allow you to pull back and look over years and decades to get a wider timeline and a fresh perspective. A long-term chart view will show you if the stock is just taking a breather before it reaches a new high.

- Charts will show you when a stock is breaking down. You'll see that the trend line is oversold or is headed in that direction.

- Charts show you when a stock is being squeezed and is about to break out.

- Charts let you know when it's time to strongly consider whether your stock is a keeper or if you are better off getting out completely.

- Charts allow you to keep your cool and take the emotion out of your decisions.

Time For a Change

You need to know what to do if a core holding goes way up or down in price. Investing in the market is part science, part art. Not understanding these two concepts can give a lot of investors trouble. They want to hold on — sometimes until the bitter end. The goal is to limit your losses and increase your profits over time. That's why we discussed not having all your eggs in one basket, and to diversify holdings in sectors and multiple industries – and even then you may not prevent a loss. Go back to your Four Key Cloud Elements and evaluate the stock as if it were a new purchase. The most important question you must ask yourself is: **Would you buy the stock as a new investment?** If your answer is "yes," then now is a good time to actually dip in and pick up another block of the stock.

If your answer is "no," it may be time to move on! Consider discussing the tax implications with your tax and financial advisor before selling a stock. He or she might offer a sound suggestion you would not want to miss out on. Park your proceeds in a cash account and take a breather until you're ready to make a new investment.

Let It Run

A stock that's moving higher, leave it alone – let it run. Move away from your computer and watch it. Sometimes a stock that runs up quickly needs time to catch up with itself. You may want to sit back and take a breather too. Think of a mountain climber. She doesn't just race up the mountain; she stops and rests and then sets out again. Stay the course if your stock is just taking time to rest before its next move higher. If you're concerned that it has run its course, pull up a Bollinger Band chart. Review a 5-day, 10-day, and 3-month chart to gauge when it may start to move again. You may also want to take this opportunity to add to your position. Check out market sentiment and news. The lull in the stock may just be a normal seasonal cycle or an overreaction to news in the sector or market.

Let It Go

Deciding when to sell is difficult for a lot of investors who are emotionally attached to their stock. Use your charts. They speak louder than words! Sometimes you have to look at all the reasons a stock is going down and make a decision.

If you do decide to sell because the stock has peaked and is coming off the top of its price range, you may not get the absolute top price when you sell. That's okay. You're not trying to time this or the market.

When a stock price is falling you have to protect yourself! After you have looked at the chart, if the Bollinger Bands are getting wide, putting downward pressure on the stock, you may need to consider some protection, moving out of some, or all of the position.

You have several options at this point:

- Sell all or a portion of your shares as a **"market"** order.
  - This order will process immediately at the next available price.
- Sell all or a portion of your shares as a **"stop"** or a **"stop-limit"** — **"day"** or **"good-till-cancelled"** order.
  - A "stop" order allows you to set a price point. Once the stock price hits the dollar figure you set, it will trigger an immediate sell at the next available price, which could be lower than the "stop" price.
  - A "stop-limit" becomes a "limit" order after a "stop" has been triggered. The order waits to be filled until it's triggered again by reaching your limit price. At that point

it may not be filled right away, if the stock price is lower than what you ordered. The "limit" side of this order will be held in the system until the share price is available. This means, your "limit" order may be filled as the stock price is on the way back up, or never!

- o A "day" order expires if it has not been filled on the day it's entered.
- o A "good-till-cancelled" order is in the system for several months or until the order has been filled.

- Sell all or a portion of your shares in round lot's (increments of 100 shares) using a number of option strategies.

- Hold all or a portion of the shares.

- Buy more shares at the lower price after completing a full review.

After a sizeable move up or down in the stock price, it may be a good time to check the Bollinger Bands to see if a new breakout is coming. If you need help confirming a squeeze, or a new trend, I suggest you get in touch with your financial advisor, or use your exclusive offer code in the "About the Author" section.

Stormy Weather — Bumpy Markets

Know what you are investing in and understand that there are several levels of risk. There is a risk the stock price will go lower instead of higher. There is a risk of a "market event" that takes the entire market down, like a recession. Even the weather can have an effect on the market. There's the risk that management and those who are the visionary leaders in the company will leave, or at some point pass away. The risk here is not knowing, who will replace them. There is a currency risk if you are buying companies that earn money from overseas investments. There is risk with rising inflation and higher commodity prices. There are risks in life and in investing. There will be many challenges along the way. It's part of the process.

Diversification is an important element for smoothing out the market bumps and fluctuating interest rates that will come along over time. Spreading your investments around and not having all your money in one or two stocks is just a better way to go. However, even those investors who do a good job diversifying are not completely safe. If there was a large-scale market event like another recession, a major earthquake, or — God forbid — an attack from an enemy, stocks, bonds, gold, oil, you name it, could go down in value.

When the overall market moves up and down — *as it always will* — investors who have the financial means, time, and emotional stability to weather the market storm may be better off mentally and possibly financially. I have said a thousand times, from the moment you buy a stock it will go lower, and it will go higher than what you paid for it. The goal is to buy low and sell high. If the stock market upsets your stomach or keeps you awake at night, step back and reassess your reason for investing.

There is no cookie cutter or magic formula for success. It takes time, knowing what to look for, and what to look out for, and even then some don't get it right. When in doubt, check with a financial professional who can help guide you through market storms that will surely happen. A financial advisor who understands the market and knows your personal needs can be one of your best investments. You can always use your exclusive **offer code** located in the "About the Author" section.

PART IV:

THE PROCESS

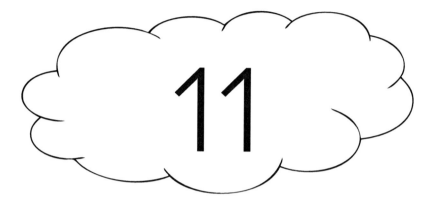

CLOUD CONTROL

"Youth may savor the challenge and promise of the future."

WALT DISNEY

There are new opportunities and new challenges both in the market and in cloud computing companies. Knowing what needs to be done and staying on top of market developments and new opportunities is essential to a healthy financial portfolio. You need to stay current on your holdings and be able to do analysis quickly so it doesn't suck up all your time. You need to see when changes should be made.

This requires budgeting a little time each day. Once you set this up correctly, it won't take but a few minutes a day — and weekly, it will take less than the time it takes you to wash, dry, and put away a load of clothes… provided you do your own laundry.

To keep current, you need to know the price movements in your core cloud companies — those you own and those on your consideration list. I suggest you set up a portfolio of your "cloud core" holdings and your "wish and watch" list. For those of you who have a brokerage account, this should already be done for you on the stocks you own, but you still want to create a core cloud "wish and watch" list.

Portfolio Check-in

Your daily goal is to check in with your portfolio. Not to be a day trader, but to be mindful of what's going on with each company's stock. You can make your own spreadsheet, but that's going to be time-consuming. Here are some ideas to help make monitoring your portfolio a daily habit:

I recommend monitoring your stocks online. You can do this at no cost or through a paid service. Your time is valuable and you don't want to be fussing over putting data in a spreadsheet every day. Having it done for you is the only way to go. You can keep it very basic, and often you have options to customize it.

- If you have a Yahoo or Google account, it's easy to create a stock watch list.

- For those of you working with a full-service brokerage firm or a discount company, online access showing your holding pages and unrealized gains and losses should come with your account.

- If you use a paid charting service, they usually offer customized portfolios as part of your service agreement.

Setting Up an Account

For those of you who have never bought or sold a stock on your own, you can open a full-service brokerage account and, with the help of a financial advisor, get started or, if you are a do-it-yourself kind of investor, head over to an online company.

Full Service

It's a good idea before you begin any investment program to seek out the help of a professional investment advisor. It may save you time and money down the road. Every financial advisor comes with his or her own unique set of experiences and expertise. You don't want to buy bread from the butcher when you want to eat beef! If you want to own stocks and, more specifically, cloud computing companies, you won't go to an insurance agent who only sells life insurance.

You want to work with a financial advisor who has a series 7 license, is experienced in all types of stock market conditions, and has the ability to do research. (You should still do your own thinking and homework.) He or she doesn't have to be a tech-guru. I don't even think such an advisor exists. Technology changes so fast, that it's hard for even those working in the industry to keep up. As long as you can find an advisor who can do his or her own thinking (like you), who sees the vision, and who gets tech on some level, he or she should be able to guide your investment portfolio. A full-service broker can be an excellent person to help you, especially for those of you who work alone.

Recognize that not all firms are the same. Some require a minimum net worth and a minimum "investable" net worth before they will see you. Others have a more flexible open-door policy and are happy to help clients who are just starting out and who may not have a lot of funds to invest.

Online — Paper Trades

There are several online trading companies that will allow you to get started using **paper trades**. In a paper trade, you don't actually use money or own stock. It's a way to get your feet wet and use make-believe "play money." Once you're comfortable with how the process and technology works, you can switch over to real money and off you go.

From time to time, online companies make offers to new clients. Incentives can range from a set number of discounted trades to cash on your account. Do a search for online brokers and check out a few before you make a decision, and be sure to get a complete list of their add-on services and fees.

Set up news alerts on each of your cloud companies and those on your future buy list. Keep up-to-date on daily price changes and news on each company, and use a central location to store the information so it's easy to monitor. As I mentioned before, you want a process that is easy and won't take up all your time. You need relevant information on your holdings and those on your "wish and watch" list as it crosses the new wires.

The easiest way to accomplish this is a free "alert" service from either Yahoo or Google.

- When there is news — even the slightest mention of your company — an alert will be sent out to you with the information.

- Adjust the settings to receive alerts daily (all in one e-mail) or immediately, as they are released.

Yahoo Alerts

To set up a Yahoo Alert, start by going to the **Yahoo Finance** page and typing in the stock symbol you want to set an alert on. Once the page comes up, scroll all the way down to the bottom right side of the page. You will see the words "**Toolbox.**"

Click on: A **Set Alert for.** Once you click on this, it will take you to a log-in page.

Log in or Create New Account

If you have a Yahoo account, log in. If you don't have a Yahoo ID, click on **Create New Account.** You will be asked to choose a user name and password, and then it will take you to the **Stock Watch Alert** page to start putting in the stock symbols and setting the alert criteria for each company. You will need to fill in the price and percentage ranges for each stock. You will be able at any time to edit, update, or delete stock information.

Yahoo stores this information in their data centers; you are not required to download any software, and the only thing you need is an Internet connection. How this works is pretty straightforward. If the stock price falls or rises by a dollar amount or a percentage you set, the service sends you an alert.

Before you leave Yahoo Alerts, scroll to the bottom and hit [**SAVE**].

NOTE: You can set the Yahoo alerts to notify you as they happen or once a day. You can also set the time of day that alerts are sent out to fit into your schedule.

My Alerts — Keywords

While still in **Yahoo** you can set an alert on **keywords** and get up-to-the-second updates delivered to your e-mail, Yahoo Messenger, or mobile device. If you want to see any news that contains keywords, all you do is type those keywords under the tab **My Alerts**, and create an **Alert on Keywords**.

Next, still in **Keywords,** add in the stock symbols of those companies you want news updates and alerts on. Most news articles will add the stock symbol in their stories, so that makes it easy for you to type them in. This is an effective way to manage your stocks and your time. Now you're working with cloud computing at its best!

NOTE: If you use Microsoft Outlook, you may want to **create a folder** for each stock you follow. **Create a rule** to have news alerts automatically filter to this folder. It keeps your inbox neat and they are all stored in one place so nothing is overlooked or misplaced.

High-Tech Help

If you're still a bit fuzzy on just how to set up a stock portfolio or alerts online, help is here. You know the old saying, "Time is money"? I am going to save you time. For making the commitment to "own the clouds," I have posted on my website (www.blonskij.com) complimentary reference guides. These step-by-step instructions will get you up to speed on creating and tracking your portfolio. You will learn how to add, edit, and remove stocks, and you'll also be able to keep your information fresh and up-to-date.

Complimentary Reference Guides

Your complimentary reference guides are located at **www.blonskij.com** under the tab **CLOUDS**. You will want to "bookmark" this site and check back monthly to get new guides and updates. Download these now and get started right away:

- Setting Up A Yahoo Stock Portfolio. Your Step-by-Step On-line Guide.
- Setting Up Yahoo Alerts. Your Step-by-Step On-line Guide.

1. **Is there breaking news on your stock or a large price move up or down?**

Take a few minutes to check the headlines and go back and chart the stock.

- Run a "basic" 1-day and 5-day chart.

- Is there enough volume coming into the stock to push this into a full-blown move? Look at the daily volume and compare it to past trading days. Is it in a normal range or way outside its norm?

- Run a Bollinger Band on a 90-day and a 6-month chart. Look for signs of a run in the stock (wide-open bands or bands beginning to open).

- Look for price changes both in dollar moves and percentage moves and compare this to your last price and projected target (**1y Target Est.**). You're looking for wide swings that could sound an alarm that something is up.

2. **Should the charts indicate a negative bias and the bands show they are getting wider, go back to these primary questions**:

- Is the stock taking a breather before moving higher?

- Is the stock still dominant and a leader in its sector?

- Has the company's stock quality declined or has their competition gotten better?

- Was the news source from inside the company or an outside source?

- Was the source reliable?

- Does the stock still have the ability to make a profit going forward in the next year?

- Is there a trend starting or is this a normal business cycle?

- Does the stock appear to be in a strong position or falling behind?

- How much pressure is being put on the stock share price? Up or down? *Use your Bollinger Band chart to identify pressure.*

- Given the opportunity, would you buy the stock as a new investment?

- When in doubt, get a second opinion.

Rolling Clouds

I firmly believe that cloud computing will be recognized and embraced as the "new normal." The evolution of our species is unfolding as the secrets of the universe and technology are revealed. In your research on cloud computing companies thus far, you have expanded your universe. You're more aware of how your life is going to change with advances coming from new discoveries, new science, and advanced technology. You have a head start. As your family, friends and co-workers start sizing up this sector of the market, you will already have your feet on the ground and your head in the clouds. When your peers' awareness ignites, step back and take it all in.

Investment Tips

The investment tips I am about to share with you can be applied to every stock in every industry and sector…and especially cloud computing companies. Investing in clouds follows the same basic guidelines and investment rules as all financial investments.

Tip # 1: Follow the Money

"Follow the money" – **follow a trend.** Supply and demand, buying and selling shares, moves stock prices higher and lower. When mutual fund managers, institutional money managers, and the mega-rich start buying up shares in a stock, the daily volume increases, and "big money" is on the move. As buy-side volume increases, it's a sign that investors are pouring money into a stock, and they're all looking for the same things: to own a well run business, and to make **a profit.**

You need and want to be able to recognize when "big money" is buying, and as a trend is forming. When you're able to spot "big money" on the move, and get in front of it, "big money" will be a very good friend. On the flip side, when "big money" moves out of a stock, especially in a hurry – **look out!**

One way to follow what "big money" is doing is to look at the volume of shares being bought and sold. Start by pulling up a Yahoo chart on the stock. Look at the daily volume on a 5-day to a one year chart, keeping in mind any seasonal cycles.

Next click on the tab **COMPANY [Key Statistics]** *(Exhibit No.1, D:2)*. On the far right side of the page you'll see **Trading Information.** You're looking for the second section down labeled: **Shared Statistics.** This looks at the average volume from the last ten days and the past three months. As you compare this older data to the number of shares currently being traded, you should be able to get a pretty good idea if there is an increase in the demand for your cloud company.

Another way to help you see what "big money" is up to is from a paid service. I use a paid service from Investools. One of the many features they offer is tracking "big money." On their site you'll see a color-coded line graph showing "big-money" interest from zero, which is no interest, up to one hundred, which is the highest level of interest. With all the publically traded cloud computing companies out there, you'll need to be able to access their stock information quickly, which is why I use their site.

Take a moment and watch this video from Investools, and see why I find their service of value when it comes to analysis and "big money."

http://www.investools.com/content/website/demos2/toolboxTour.html

Cloudy Skies

There will be times when "big money" gets it wrong. A trend that's new or just getting started could break down and change direction on you. Even if your research and instincts are correct, an unexpected announcement or market event could drive the stock price lower. So you need to be alert and keep an eye on the stocks you follow.

A long-term trend is a stronger indicator. A long-term trend is based on months and years. That's why day trading is considered risky. Day-trading price movements are limited to hours or minutes. Your goal as an investor is to be able to identify and own well-run businesses — companies that have visionary management that can innovate and create products and services that will lead them into the future. You want to look for strong balance sheets, good cash flow, and rising earning growth. Businesses that dominate and innovate! You want the companies that are moving the clouds with new ways of doing business, and that are changing the landscape of homes and offices globally. You're looking for the 800-pound gorillas, and the up-and-coming bright stars!

Following the money is one way to ride the wind currents blowing behind the clouds.

Tip # 2: Think It Through and Follow Through

Making investment decisions to buy or sell stocks requires you to have a clear picture of the company and a good amount of facts. You need a sound basis for all your investment decisions. You would never think of buying a home without walking through the kitchen, checking out the yard, or seeing what repairs are needed. You would collect all the data, check the price, make comparisons, and then make an informed decision. The same is true for buying financial investments like stocks.

As an investor, you need to think accurately and *think it through* based on known facts, good judgment, and some good-old common sense. Being able to separate facts from opinions and prejudices is not easy. The facts will stand on their own legs — like reading a chart. If the MACD and

StochRSI are showing a negative trend, no matter how badly you want that stock to go up you are more than likely going to have to wait it out. The more realistic short-term trend would be to go lower…at least for a while. One thing you do know is that a chart is not going to debate you. Charts do not have an opinion or a bias. They are what they are: a non-emotional, mathematical calculation based on past, real data, provided by the price movements and several other technical elements. They can help you make an investment decision.

Good judgment and common sense are more difficult to sort out. These, in part, are a result of your experiences and how well you've learned from your mistakes and successes. Be careful when you tune in to TV or radio financial shows, and read blogs or financial newsletters, that you don't fall for slanted opinions – good or bad.

Diligent thinkers learn the facts and then listen to their better judgment. They are cautious, but not afraid. You tell small children that the stove is hot and not to touch it. Then you teach them how to cook. Like with the stove, you can get burned investing. But you can also make a profit. Take, for example, all the upside-down homeowners who bought at the top of the housing bubble and are in foreclosure. They got burned big time. Now, look at all of the first-time homebuyers who are getting super values today buying those very same homes. I am not suggesting timing the housing or stock market. I am suggesting you think it through before you buy. Once you have done your research, follow your better judgment.

Thin Air

A follow-through could be a decision not to make a purchase, just as it could be to make one. You need to sort out all the noise from Wall Street and focus your energy on finding those clouds with silver linings.

Wouldn't it be nice if there were such a thing as a "one-size-fits-all" investment program? Actually, no! If it were that simple and straightforward, the returns would be pitiful. It takes a sharp eye and a keen mind to get in step with — or better yet, one step ahead of — a solid trend.

Last Words

You have new insights and tools. You're as ready as you'll ever be. You have a good idea of what to look for and how to dig through all the layers. It's time to get to work!

"The way to get started is to quit talking and begin doing."

WALT DISNEY

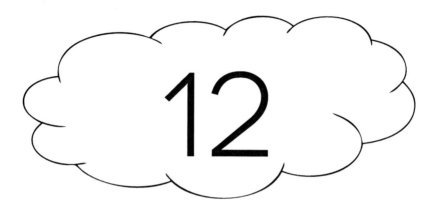

TRACKING CLOUDS
BLUEPRINT

"It will never cease to be a living blueprint of the future, where people actually live a life they can't find anywhere else in the world."

WALT DISNEY

Low-Tech or High-Tech

Keeping track of your clouds is easy when you have a system. I strongly suggest you go high-tech and use a charting service that provides instant delivery of news and price alerts. One that gives you a number of chart views and a closing summary of your portfolio holdings. However, sometimes the "old-fashioned" ways, i.e., pen and paper, are hard to break. If you decide to go low-tech, you'll still need to set price and news alerts to be delivered to your smartphone or e-mail.

First Day — Blueprint

Go to **www.Blonskij.com** and under the tab: **CLOUDS** print up the free step-by-step on-line guides for: "**Setting Up A Yahoo Stock Portfolio**" and "**Setting Up Yahoo Stock Alerts.**"

_____Set-up: **Yahoo Finance: Toolbox [Set an Alert] > Stock Watch.** This will help you monitor daily stock price and percentage movements. It's a huge time saver!

_____Set-up: **Yahoo Finance: [My Alerts] > Keyword/News.** This will allow you to receive fast breaking news, announcements, and to set-up multiple searches.

_____Set-up: **Yahoo Finance: Create a Portfolio / Add to Portfolio.** This will let you to mark the stocks you want to see in a daily closing stock summary.

_____Never miss a financial show by tuning in or programming your TV recorder.

_____Subscribe to RSS feeds (Really Simply Syndications.) This is an effective way to track bloggers and get a feel for what's being said. When you subscribe to RSS feeds the blog article is send directly to you.

_____Follow Twitter feeds that can add value to your investment process.

_____Commit to a couple of trial subscriptions to financial e-zines and newsletters.

_____Open a brokerage (full-service) or online account.

_____Check with your account provider regarding web access.

Daily — Blueprint

After the market closes, check your portfolio and review your holdings. Once you have set up a Yahoo account for alerts, they will send you a daily **"Stock Summary"** of some or all of your stocks. These Yahoo reports will save you hours every day.

Keep an eye on the following information: price per share on the open and close, the low and high for the day, and the volume. You want to look for price swings and how heavy or light the trading (volume) was during the day. Factor this into how the overall market did as well.

There are a number of stock indexes you can follow. Some indexes track just a few stocks. An example of this is the Dow. The Dow follows thirty stocks. My suggestion to you is to follow the S&P500 index, which follows the five hundred largest companies publicly traded in the U.S. This index will give you a wider sample of how stocks are moving in the overall market. Once you decide which index to follow, you'll want to review the daily open and close and the index low and high for the day. Tracking this alongside your stocks may give you additional insight. It may help you determine if your stock is out-of-step with the market, which could be a signal something was out of the ordinary — in a good or bad way.

_____Review: **Stock Summary**. Look for price gaps and compare the day's closing price to the prior day's last trade price. This data will be sent to your inbox, mobile device, or as a Yahoo instant message. **Yahoo Finance: Create an Alert > Stock Summary.**

_____ Review: News, blogs, and company announcements sent via **Keyword/News** alerts. This data will be sent to your inbox, mobile device, or as a Yahoo instant message. **Yahoo Finance: My Alerts.**

_____Look at the **headlines** and **breaking news** stories of the day. Pay attention to any stocks you follow. **Yahoo Finance: [NEWS & INFO]** *(Exhibit No.1, C:1).*

_____Watch the financial shows you taped earlier in the day.

_____Look through your Twitter and RSS feeds from the day.

Weekly – Blueprint

The Buzz from Wall Street

_____Review: **Yahoo Finance [NEWS & INFO]** *(Exhibit No.1, C:1:, C:2).* See what's being said about the company, management, and product line-up going forward.

_____Tap into what bloggers are saying. Try to pick up on positive or negative chatter.

Outside Scoop

_____Review: Analyst opinions. **Yahoo Finance [ANALYST COVERAGE]** *(Exhibit No. 1, E:1)*

_____Review: Analyst estimates. **Yahoo Finance [ANALYST COVERAGE]** *(Exhibit No. 1, E:2)*

Inside Scoop

_____Review: Insider transactions. **Yahoo Finance [OWNERSHIP]** *(Exhibit No. 1, F:2)*

Charts

If you are using a charting service, this will be a snap to review. Just log in and pull up your portfolio in a "summary" chart view. This will allow you to see thumbnails of all your stocks. Look for unusual spikes in volume, bands squeezing or getting wider, and if any of your positions are oversold or overbought. Run the following:

_____Basic chart

_____Bollinger Band

_____MACD

_____StochRSI

_____Check the Put/Call Ratios from the CBOE www.cboe.com

_____Look for "Big Money" Volume moving in-or-out. Yahoo Finance [COMPANY] **Key Statistics** *(Exhibit No. 1, D:2)* and **Trading Information** (right side of the page) ▼ **Shared Statistics**.

_____Update, review, and edit stock price alerts and percentage changes as needed. **Yahoo FINANCE: Create An Alert.**

Quarterly – Blueprint

Earnings Release

_____Quarterly earnings report: **Yahoo Finance [NEWS & INFO] Company Events**: Set a ⏰ **Reminder Alert,** *Upcoming Earnings Announcements*. Once you've set up alerts on each of your stocks, you will receive quarterly e-mails or texts when they have reported their earning and future outlook. Be aware of any negative changes.

Competitors and Insiders

_____Review: Top competitors and compare them side-by-side: **Yahoo Finance [COMPANY]** *(Exhibit No. 1, D:3)*

_____ Review: Insider transactions to see what management is doing with their shares. **Yahoo Finance [OWNERSHIP]** *(Exhibit No. 1, F:2)*

Cloud Index

_____Compare the companies in the Cloud Computing Stocks (*CLOUD) Index at Tickerspy. Here is their link: **http://www.tickerspy. com/index/Cloud-Computing-Stocks**.

Once on the website, click "**Track This Index**." If you are not registered on the site, you'll be directed to a page to create a user name and password, enter your e-mail address, and choose from a number of ways to get updates; and best of all, it's free!

_____Check for new additions or deletions, and how the overall index has performed relative to the market.

Financials

_____Review: Income statement. **Yahoo Finance [FINANCIALS]** *(Exhibit No. 1, G:1)*

_____Review: Balance sheet. **Yahoo Finance [FINANCIALS]** *(Exhibit No. 1, G:2)*

_____Review: Cash flow. **Yahoo Finance [FINANCIALS]** *(Exhibit No. 1, G:3)*

Annual — Blueprint

Annual Report and Letter to Shareholders

Once a year, companies publish their annual report and a cover letter to shareholders. Shareholders receive this package in the mail. If you don't own the stock, this information is still available to you. From the company website, go to the tab **Investor Relations** and pull up the annual report.

Years ago, I learned how to quickly scan these. Start with the letter to shareholders. Like any good author, they tell you in the first paragraph how they did. The rest of the letter is either to pat themselves on the back with lots of wonderful numbers showing you how great they are, or to defend themselves, squirming, trying to explain away why they missed this and that over the past year. My rule of thumb is to read the first and last paragraph of the letter to shareholders. If I need more information, I crack open the report and review the company's operations, balance sheet, and income statement.

If at any time you'd like a second opinion, feel free to use your **CLOUD9** offer.

9 Cloud Guidelines for Investors

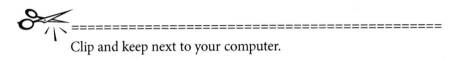

Clip and keep next to your computer.

1. Look for and own well-run businesses. As a stockholder, you are an "owner" in the company.

    - If the company does poorly, the stock will suffer.

    - If the company does well, the value of the company can increase over time.

2. Be logical – not emotional. Keep a cool head. It's business. Not personal.

3. Review and edit Yahoo FINANCE: Stock Watch.

4. Review and edit Yahoo FINANCE: My Alerts > Keyword/News Alerts.

5. Keep an eye out for the unexpected and unusual. You just never know what's floating around.

6. Don't guess. Get professional guidance.

7. Soak up information. Learn more every day.

    - Tech posts from the Consumer Electronic Association (CEA).

    - Watch and record financial shows.

    - Read e-zines, subscribe to newsletters, and check-out trial offers.

    - Tap into RSS feeds from top financial folks.

    - Follow Twitter tech and financial posts.

    - Attend a technology conference or trade show.

8. Run a chart before you buy or sell a stock.

9. Enjoy the journey and have fun!

ABOUT THE AUTHOR

Joyce Blonskij
Named a FIVE-STAR Wealth Manager^{SM}**

Joyce Blonskij began her career in banking, quickly working her way to becoming vice president and branch manager at a major local bank. After nearly 10 years in the banking industry, she transitioned into what she calls "the world of high finance," and in 1985, Joyce became an investment advisor at Dean Witter Reynolds, Inc. For more than 18 years, she was a mentor to other women advisors, managed a large client-based practice, and was recognized by her peers at the highest level of achievement for her work with the title of senior vice president. In 2003, she opened her own financial services firm, Blonskij Financial Services, Inc., now located in Fair Oaks, California.

Joyce writes a financial blog you can read at www.BrillianceByBlonskij. com, and is recognized as an experienced financial speaker, offering cutting-edge, highly informative content for a broad audience.

Joyce graduated from California State University, Sacramento, and holds a certificate with the American College for Estate Planning Professionals. She is a native of Sacramento, California, and lives with her husband John Blonskij, their English Springer Spaniel, and two cats. They have one daughter, Stephanie.

Joyce Blonskij – President, Blonskij Financial Services, Inc.
Financial Advisor | Author and Speaker
e-mail: Joyce@Blonskij.com • website: www.blonskij.com
7840 Madison Avenue, Suite 107 • Fair Oaks, California 95628
Toll-Free: 1 (866) 339-6400

Special Offer Code: CLOUD9

This exclusive code is your direct access to Joyce Blonskij. If you get stuck and have a question, need help verifying a trend, or are looking for a second opinion, use this special offer code "**CLOUD9**" in the subject line of your e-mail.

Send your e-mail to: joyce@blonskij.com

Book – Joyce Blonskij

To inquire about availability and to book Joyce to speak to your group or at your next conference, e-mail her at: joyce@blonskij.com

Follow – Joyce Blonskij

- **Blonskij Financial Services:** www.Blonskij.com

- **Joyce's author and speaker site:** www.JoyceBlonskij.com

- **Joyce's financial blog:** www.BrillianceByBlonskij.com

- **LinkedIn:** www.linkedin.com/in/JoyceBlonskij

- **Twitter:** www.twitter.com/JoyceBlonskij

- **FIVE-STAR Wealth Manager:** www.fivestarprofessional.com/2012/view_profile.php/Joyce/Blonskij/41439

FIVE-STAR Wealth Manager^{SM} – Disclosure Statement

To receive the Five-Star Wealth Manager award, individuals must satisfy a series of eligibility and evaluation criteria associated with wealth managers who provide services to clients. Recipients are identified through research conducted by industry peers and firms. Third party rankings and recognitions from rating services or publications are not indicative of past or future investment performance. For more information, go to www. fivestarprofessional.com.

Broker/Dealer – Disclosure Statement

Registered Representative, Securities offered through Cambridge Investment Research, Inc., a Broker/Dealer, Member FINRA/SIPC. Investment Advisor Representative, Cambridge Investment Advisors, Inc., a Registered Investment Advisor. Blonskij Financial Services, Inc. & Cambridge are not affiliated.

Hold Harmless Statement

As each individual situation is different, specific questions should be addressed to an appropriate professional to ensure that your needs are carefully evaluated. This book is sold with the understanding that neither the Author, Broker/Dealer (Cambridge Investment Research) or Publisher is engaged in rendering legal, accounting, or other professional services by publishing this book. The Author, Broker/Dealer and Publisher specifically disclaim any liability, loss, or risk which is incurred as a result, directly or indirectly, of the use and application of any of the contents of this work.

Option Disclosure

Options involve risk and are not suitable for all investors. Before buying or selling an option, a person must receive a copy of Characteristics and Risks of Standardized Options (ODD). Copies of the ODD are available from your broker. The information in this text that discussed options, was provided solely for general education and informational purposes and should not be considered complete, precise, or current.

Web Links – Disclosure Statement

The information being provided is strictly as a courtesy. When you link to any of these web sites provided herein, Cambridge Investment Research and Blonskij Financial Services makes no representation as to the completeness or accuracy of information provided at these sites. Nor is the company liable for any direct or indirect technical or system issues or any consequences arising out of your access to or your use of third-party technologies, sites, information, and programs made available through these sites.

ACKNOWLEDGMENTS

Many people helped get *Own the Clouds* published. Todd Lay got the ball rolling. I met Todd at BNI (Business Network International), where he shared his new book. Six months later, Todd insisted I take five minutes in the spotlight at our Sacramento Speakers Network Meetup Group to share my writing challenges on a report about clouds that I had been preparing for my clients. When I finished getting input from the group and sat down, at that moment I knew this book had to be written. Todd, I will be forever thankful.

I'm particularly grateful for the structural and creative input I got from my book coach Allan Fahden — thank you! Amberly Finarelli, you are one heck of an editor and Marjorie Blum for your second pair of fresh eyes. Stephanie Chandler and John Rizzo, you gave me guidance and the courage to write. Thank you so much.

My back office staff at Cambridge Investment Research: Bruce Dickson, Todd Clark and my team in Iowa, especially Dan VanWinkle. You are all great to work with! Thank you for helping make this book a reality.

To the amazing women in my life: Hilda Mae Lavergne, my dearest friend, who has been working and standing by my side for three decades. I love you, Hilda. Nataliya Condriuc and Chloe, you bring joy into my life. Thank you for being there whenever I needed your help. My lifelong best friend, Rebecca ("R") Canale, you saved me days of work on this book! I love having you in my life. Not only are you smart and beautiful, you're my personal shopper, and you wear me out! My BGF, Sonja Craighton. Cross this off my bucket list. Amanda Decker, my soul sister and advocate. You help keep me accountable, and I thank you for this. Dr. Caroline Wadlin, M.D. (www.PreventBurnOutNow.com) and Sue Peppers, my fellow authors and dear friends, fate has brought us together. Thank you all for your help, encouragement and believing in me.

To all my mentors and mentees over the years, I learned from your successes and mistakes, along with some of my own. I appreciate all the lessons you bestowed upon me.

To my amazing and wonderful clients, I wrote this book for you! Thank you for being my extended family and a huge part of my life.

In loving memory of my first and only Wall Street manager: Wayne Gilliam. For eighteen years we fought like siblings, and I loved him like a big brother. Wayne and I were both "bulls in a china store." His words of wisdom continue to echo in my head.

My dearest daughter, Stephanie, I always thought you'd be the first author in the family, not me. I hope this book inspires you to write your own story. I know it would be a doozy!

To the love of my life, thank you for allowing me to bury myself in this and all the projects I have put my heart and soul into. All I can say is, thank God you can cook, or we'd starve to death! And to my other love, Daniel Boone the bird dog, who slept and nestled under my feet the entire time I was writing. He never once complained when he missed our walks. *"He's a good boy."*

Thank you.

Now let's go out and *Own the Clouds!*

GIVING BACK

In the spirit of giving back, I am delighted to donate a portion of the author proceeds from *Own the Clouds* to help infants and children recover quicker from serious and life threatening injuries, illnesses, and diseases to those organizations that provide for parents and family to be close-at-hand while their children are in the hospital.

The medical community agrees, children surrounded with the love and support of a caring family respond better to treatments. Kids get better faster when mom and dad are there to hold their hand, and tell them, "*It will be all right.*"

Clouds Charity

My primary charity of choice is: **The Kiwanis Family House.** They have been recognized internationally for their efforts to keep family members closely connected to their sick, injured, and recovering children. I have personally seen the effects this facility has on families, who would do *anything* to be near their child. And frankly, they need our support.

Clouds Helping Children

With your purchase of *Own the Clouds*, you are helping children heal.

Kiwanis Family House

To make a personal donation, volunteer your services, get more information or to subscribe to their monthly newsletter, "House Talk" — visit their web site at: **www.kiwanisfamilyhouse.org**

EXHIBIT NO. 1

Own the Clouds

Summary Page – Yahoo Finance

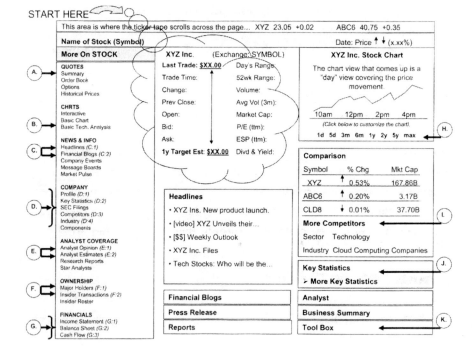

START HERE

This area is where the ticker tape scrolls across the page... XYZ 23.05 +0.02   ABC6 40.75 +0.35

Name of Stock (Symbol) — Date: Price ↑ ↓ (x.xx%)

More On STOCK

A.
QUOTES
Summary
Order Book
Options
Historical Prices

B.
CHRTS
Interactive
Basic Chart
Basic Tech. Analysis

C.
NEWS & INFO
Headlines *(C:1)*
Financial Blogs *(C:2)*
Company Events
Message Boards
Market Pulse

D.
COMPANY
Profile *(D:1)*
Key Statistics *(D:2)*
SEC Filings
Competitors *(D:3)*
Industry *(D:4)*
Components

E.
ANALYST COVERAGE
Analyst Opinion *(E:1)*
Analyst Estimates *(E:2)*
Research Reports
Star Analysts

F.
OWNERSHIP
Major Holders *(F:1)*
Insider Transactions *(F:2)*
Insider Roster

G.
FINANCIALS
Income Statement *(G:1)*
Balance Sheet *(G:2)*
Cash Flow *(G:3)*

XYZ Inc.   (Exchange:SYMBOL)

Last Trade: **$XX.00**   Day's Range:
Trade Time: 52wk Range:
Change: Volume:
Prev Close: Avg Vol (3m):
Open: Market Cap:
Bid: P/E (ttm):
Ask: ESP (ttm):
1y Target Est: $XX.00   Divd & Yield:

Headlines
• XYZ Ins. New product launch.
• [video] XYZ Unveils their...
• [$$] Weekly Outlook
• XYZ Inc. Files
• Tech Stocks: Who will be the...

Financial Blogs

Press Release

Reports

XYZ Inc. Stock Chart

The chart view that comes up is a "day" view covering the price movement.

10am   12pm   2pm   4pm
(Click below to customize the chart)
1d 5d 3m 6m 1y 2y 5y max   H.

Comparison

Symbol	% Chg	Mkt Cap
XYZ	↑ 0.53%	167.86B
ABC6	↑ 0.20%	3.17B
CLD8	↓ 0.01%	37.70B

More Competitors   I.
Sector   Technology
Industry Cloud Computing Companies

Key Statistics   J.
➤ **More Key Statistics**

Analyst

Business Summary

Tool Box   K.

NOTES

CHAPTER 1

1. Pony Express National Museum. Accessed June 1, 2011. http://www.ponyexpress.org/history

2. Wikipedia. "Pony Express." Founders. Accessed June 1, 2011. http://en.wikipedia.org/wiki/Pony_Express

3. Tseng, Erick. Facebook Blog. Making Mobile More Social. November 3, 2010. Accessed May 2011. http://blog.facebook.com/blog.php?post=446167297130

4. Facebook Statistics, People on Facebook. Accessed May 16, 2011. http://www.facebook.com/press/info.php?statistics

5. Facebook Gold. Edition-May 11, 2011. Facebook Surpasses 677 Million Users – More Traffic Trends and Data at Inside Facebook Gold. http://www.insidefacebook.com/2011/05/11/facebook-sur-passes-677-million-users-more-traffic-trends-and-data-at-inside-facebook-gold-may-2011-edition/

6. Watson, Thomas.1943. Famous Computer Quotes. Accessed May 16, 2011. http://ifaq.wap.org/computers/famousquotes.html

7. Gil, Paul. About.com. FAQ: How Big Is the Internet? Guide - Internet for Beginners. June 2011. Compilation of 2011 statistical projections from ClickZ and the CIA: I) Total Internet Human Usage By Country of Residence. Accessed June 2011. http://net-forbeginners.about.com/od/weirdwebculture/f/How-Big-Is-the-Internet.htm

8. Edison, Thomas. 1922. CAZITech Press Releases, Press Coverage and Quotes. Radio Craze. Accessed May 2011. http://cazitech.com/press_quotes.htm

9. Popular Mechanics, 1949. Famous Computer (mostly) Quotes. Accessed May 16, 2011. http://ifaq.wap.org/computers/famous-

quotes.html

10. Socialnomics09. Uploaded July 30, 2009. YouTube. Social Media Revolution: Is social media a fad? Accessed May 18, 2011. http://www.youtube.com/watch?v=sIFYPQjYhv8

11. Taylor, Chris. Twitter Users React to Massive Quake, Tsunami in Japan. Mashable.com. March 11, 2011. Accessed May 2011. http://mashable.com/2011/03/11/japan-tsunami/

12. Diana, Alison. Information Week. March 15, 2011.Twitter Handles 1 Billion Tweets Per Week. In honor of the microblogging site's 5th anniversary, co-founder Jack Dorsey is sharing tidbits about the company and its history. Accessed May 2011. http://www.Informationweek.com/news/internet/229301003

13. Robles, Patricio. Econsultancy Digital Makers United TM. Newspaper circulation declines, even with free copies. Accessed May 4, 2011. http://econsultancy.com/us/blog/7484-newspaper-circulation-declines-even-with-free-copies

14. CloudTweaks.com. Mar. 29, 2011. p 2. Unleashing Cloud Performance: Making the Promise of Cloud a Reality. Accessed May 2011. http://www.cloudtweaks.com/2011/03/unleashing-cloud-performance-making-the-promise

15. Gates, Bill - msnbc.com, Microsoft's Gates: Web services are "sea change" Associated Press update 11/9/2005. Accessed May 2011. http://www.msnbc.msn.com/id/9975417/

CHAPTER 2

1. Helft, Miguel. Ballmer: The PC Will Continue to Thrive. The New York Times. Business. Innovation. Technology. Society. Bits. June 2, 2010. Steven J Jobs predicted. Accessed May 2011. http://bits.blogs.nytimes.com/tag/ballmer/

2. The History of Encyclopedia Britannica. Wikipedia.org. Accessed May 2011. http://en.wikipedia.org/wiki/Encyclop%C3%A6dia_

Britannica

3. Qualman, Erik. Over 50% of the World's Population is Under 30 – Social Media on the Rise. Socialnomics. April 13, 2010. Accessed May 2011. http://www.socialnomics.net/2010/04/13/over-50-of-the-worlds-population-is-under-30-social-media-on-the-rise/

4. Perez, Sarah. ReadWriteWeb. College Stops Giving Students New Email Accounts: Start Of New Trend? November 20, 2008. Accessed May 2011. http://www.readwriteweb.com/archives/college_stops_giving_students_new_email_accounts.php

5. Jones, Russell. Senior Citizens Fastest-Growing Group on Facebook. July 9, 2010. Accessed May 2011. http://www.5newsonline.com/news/kfsm-news-facebook-senior-citizens,0,5956152.story

6. Phelps, David. HR and Facebook: It's complicated. Star Tribune. Updated: Feb. 7, 2010. Accessed May 2011. http://www.startribune.com/business/83725197.html

7. Qualman, Erik. Is Social Media a Fad or the biggest shift since the Industrial Revolution? Welcome to the Social Media Revolution. Socialnomics. August 11, 2009. Accessed May 2011. http://www.socialnomics.net/2009/08/11/statistics-show-social-media-is-bigger-than-you-think/

8. Qualman, Erik. Is Social Media a Fad or the biggest shift since the Industrial Revolution? Welcome to the Social Media Revolution. Socialnomics. August 11, 2009. Accessed May 2011. http://www.socialnomics.net/2009/08/11/statistics-show-social-media-is-bigger-than-you-think/

9. Baby Boomer Care. Generation Z Characteristics. Accessed May 19, 2011. http://babyboomercaretaker.com/baby-boomer/generation-z/index.html

CHAPTER 3

1. Jobs, Steve. Thinkexist.com. Steve Job quotes. Early 1970's on Atari. Accessed May 2011. http://en.thinkexist.com/quotes/steve_jobs/2.html

2. Jarboe, Greg. News at Seven has an avatar for its news anchor. Jan 8, 2007. Accessed May 2011. http://searchenginewatch.com/article/2057070/News-at-Seven-has-an-avatar-for-its-news-anchor

3. Dickens, Charles. Quotationspage.com. Quotation: A Tale of Two Cities. English Novel 1859. Accessed June 2010. http://www.quotationspage.com/quote/29595.html

4. Fisher, Irving. BrainyQuote™. Accessed April 2011. http://www.brainyquote.com/quotes/quotes/i/irvingfish193090.html

5. US bank closures hit record high in 2009. The Ultimate Business Blog. In: ECONOMY. Accessed June 2011. http://www.convr2009.com/2010/economy/us-bank-closures-hit-record-high-in-2009/

6. Amazon 2010 - Annual Report. Shipping Activity: Outbound shipping costs. Pg 26 Accessed May 2011. http://phx.corporate-ir.net/External.File?item=UGFyZW50SUQ9OTA4OTN8Q2hpbGR JRD0tMXxUeXBlPTM=&t=1

7. Hafner, Katie. New York Times. August 2, 2006. "Postal Service Finds a Friend in the Internet." Accessed June 2011. http://www.nytimes.com/2006/08/02/business/02postal.html?ei=5090&en=5 2b177f833b09c0f&ex=1312171200&pagewanted=print

8. Interactive Advertising Bureau. Economic Value of the Advertising-Supported Internet Ecosystem. Accessed June 2011. http://www.iab.net/insights_research/947883/economicvalue

9. PayScale. Salary Snapshot for Web Designer & Developer Jobs. Updated: 15 Jun 2011. Accessed June 2011. http://www.payscale.com/research/US/Job=Web_Designer_%26_Developer/Salary

10. Lison, Joseph. TCS offers cloud to small companies, hopes for billion-dollar rain. DNA. Wednesday, February 16, 2011. Accessed Feb 2011. http://www.dnaindia.com/money/report_tcs-offers-cloud-to-small-companies-hopes-for-billion-dollar-rain_1508458

11. Ballmer, Steve. The Future Is Cloudy. Forbes.com. July 29, 2010 Accessed Feb 2011. http://www.forbes.com/2010/07/28/microsoft-cloud-computers-opinions-contributors-steve-ballmer.html

12. Kaku, Dr. Michio. Quote: the video revolution is a landmark in the evolution of…" together is happening all over the world. Through video. Allowing us to connect like never before. Cisco.com. Accessed March 2011. http://together.cisco.com/??POSITION=SEM&COUNTRY_SITE=us&CAMPAIGN=HN&CREATIVE=Brand+-+Tier+1_Cisco&REFERRING_SITE=Unified&KEYWORD=cisco+systems|mkwid_eczX7NxBK_4370 50260_432txu7stz1v01134#

CHAPTER 4

1. Webster's Online Dictionary "Visionary." Synonyms: visionary. Noun. Common Expressions: visionary. Accessed May 2011. http://www.websters-online-dictionary.org/definitions/visionary?cx=partner-pub-0939450753529744%3Av0qd01-tdlq&cof=FORID%3A9&ie=UTF-8&q=visionary&sa=Search#922

2. Keizer, Gregg. First-day iPad sales top first-gen iPhone. Computerworld. April 5, 2010. Accessed May 2011.

3. Arthur, Charles and agencies. China's Internet users surpass US population. Guardian.co.uk. July 16, 2009. Accessed April 2011. http://www.guardian.co.uk/technology/2009/jul/16/china-internet-more-users-us population

4. NewMedia TrendWatch. China. Usage Patterns. Demographics.

Last Updated on Wednesday, 20 April 2011. Accessed May 2011
http://www.newmediatrendwatch.com/markets-by-country/11-long-haul/49-china

5. http://www.computerworld.com/s/article/9174836/First_day_iPad_sales_top_first_gen_iPhone

6. Froggatt, Mike. eMarketer.com. The eMarketer Blog. Why China's Mobile Video Market Might Be Poised To Explode. September 10, 2010. Accessed May 20, 2011. http://www.emarketer.com/blog/index.php/tag/mobile-usage-in-china/

7. WTEN.com. China's Internet population rise to 457 million. Albany, New York. NEWS10. Posted: Jan 18, 2011. Updated: Jan 19, 2011. Accessed May 2011. http://www.wten.com/Global/story.asp?S=13866277. http://www.cnnic.net.cn

8. Centerbeam.com. Cloud computing may reduce traffic. Industry News. Jan. 20, 2011. Accessed May 2011. http://www.centerbeam.com/news/Cloud-Computing/Report-Cloud-computing-may-reduce-traffic-CBOID74755607-GRPOID50590013/View.aspx

9. PTI Silicon India News. 34.3 percent of Chinese are hooked to Internet. Jan. 19 2011. Accessed March 2011. http://www.siliconindia.com/shownews/343_percent_of_Chinese_are_hooked_to_Internet_-nid-77660.html

10. Obama, Barack. Washingtonpost.com. May 29, 2009 Transcripts Wire. President Obama Delivers Remarks on Cyber Security Strategy. Pg 4. Accessed May 2011. http://www.washingtonpost.com/wp-dyn/content/article/2009/05/29/AR2009052901260.html

11. CYBER SPACE POLICY REVIEW. Assuring a Trusted and Resilient Information and Communications Infrastructure. Preface. Pg. i. Accessed May 2011. http://www.whitehouse.gov/assets/documents/Cyberspace_Policy_Review_final.pdf

12. National Science Foundation. Press Release 10-156. NFS Announces Future Internet Architecture Awards. Accessed May 2011. http://www.nsf.gov/news/news_summ.jsp?cntn_id=117611

13. Fulton, Jeff. eHow Contributor. Travel Agent vs. Booking Online. Accessed May 18, 2011. http://www.ehow.com/facts_5746146_travel-agent-vs_-booking-online.html

CHAPTER 5

1. Rovell, Darren. Are Super Bowl ads worth it? ESPN.com. Feb.2, 2005. Accessed May 2011. http://sports.espn.go.com/espn/page3/story?page=rovell/050203

CHAPTER 6

1. Ozzie, Ray. The Internet Services Disruption. October 28, 2005. Accessed January 2011, May 2011. http://ozzie.net/docs/the-internet-services-disruption/

PART III: The Four Key Cloud Elements

1. Funk & Wagnalls Standard Reference Encyclopedia. © 1959 Vol 6. CLOUD. pg 2207

CHAPTER 8

1. List of General Search Engines: http://en.wikipedia.org/wiki/List_of_search_engines#General

2. List of Business Search Engines: http://en.wikipedia.org/wiki/List_of_search_engines#Business

3. List of News Search Engines: http://en.wikipedia.org/wiki/List_of_search_engines#News

4. Yahoo Technology Sector List: http://biz.yahoo.com/p/technoconamed.html

5. World-newspapers.com. IT and Computer Magazines Online. Accessed May 2011. http://www.world-newspapers.com/

technology.html and http://www.world-newspapers.com/
computer.html

CHAPTER 10

1. Summa, John, CTA, PhD, Founder of OptionsNerd.com
    and HedgeMyOptions.com. Forecasting Market Direction
    With Put/Call Ratios. June 17, 2011. Accessed September
    2011. http://knowledgebase.mta.org/?fuseaction=kb.
    resource&kbDomainID=40723BA8-9D98-48B2-EE795C
    07E1B4C2FE&kbResourceID=426427DA-E058-D2AC-
    C895A55033C77614

2. StockCharts.com – ChartSchool. Moving Average Convergence-
    Divergence (MACD). Introduction. Calculation. Interpretation.
    Accessed June 2011. http://stockcharts.com/school/doku.
    php?id=chart_school:technical_indicators:movigaverage_conve

RESOURCES

B.

- Ballmer, Steve. CEO Steve Ballmer's opening keynote address at 2011 CES January 5 in Las Vegas and read transcript: http://www.microsoft.com/presspass/exec/steve/2011/01-05ces.mspx

- Blogs. Best of the Web Blogs — Business: Communications and Networking: http://blogs.botw.org/Business/Communications_and_Networking/

- Blonskij, Joyce. Author – Speaker's site: www.joyceblonskij.com

- Blonskij, Joyce. Blonskij Financial Services, Inc.: www.blonskij.com

- Blonskij, Joyce. Financial Blog: www.brilliancebyblonskij.com

- Blonskij, Joyce. FIVE-STAR Wealth Manager:

- www.fivestarprofessional.com/2011/view_profile.php/Joyce/Blonskij/41439

- Blonskij, Joyce. LinkedIn: www.linkedin.com/in/JoyceBlonskij

- Blonskij, Joyce. Twitter: www.twitter.com/JoyceBlonskij

- Bollinger Bands: www.BollingerBands.com

- Bottom-Up Investing: http://www.investopedia.com/terms/b/bottomupinvesting.asp

- http://en.wikipedia.org/wiki/Freedom_of_speech - cite_note-5#cite_note-5

- Business Networking International (BNI): http://www.bni.com/Default.aspx?tabid=626

C.

- Cambridge Investment Research Inc: http://www.joincambridge.

com/

- Chicago Board Options Exchange (CBOE): http://www.cboe.com/

- CES International website: http://www.cesweb.org/

- Chandler, Stephanie: http://www.stephaniechandler.com/

- Chandrasekaran, N. Quote: http://www.dnaindia.com/print710.php?cid=1508458

- Chicago Board Options Exchange (CBOE): www.cboe.com

- China's Savings Rate: http://finance.mapsofworld.com/savings/china/rates.html

- Cloud adoption may influence PC sales. Center Beam Industry News 1/21/2011: http://www.centerbeam.com/news/Cloud-Computing/Cloud-adoption-may-influence-PC-sales-CBOID74807916-GRPOID50590013/View.aspx

- Cloud Computing Fundamentals by Grace Walker, IT Consultant: http://www.ibm.com/developerworks/cloud/library/cl-cloudintro/

- CNBC: http://www.cnbc.com/id/15838381

- CNBC Squawk on the Street: http://en.wikipedia.org/wiki/Squawk_on_the_Street

- CNET News: http://news.cnet.com/

- Coast to Coast AM Radio with George Noory: Guest Joseph Meyer: http://www.coasttocoastam.com/guest/meyer-joe/6336

- Computer Fraud and Abuse Act 1986: http://www.justice.gov/criminal/cybercrime/ccmanual/01ccma.html

- Consumer Electronics Association (CEA): http://www.ce.org/

- Corning Inc: www.corning.com

- Corning. "A Day Made of Glass": YouTube: http://www.youtube.com/watch?v=6Cf7IL_eZ38

- Cramer, Jim. Mad Money: http://www.cramers-mad-money.com/

D.

- Daily News & Analysis (DNA): http://www.dnaindia.com/

F.

- Financial Market Trends- Economy Watch: http://www.economywatch.com/market/financial-market/trends.html
- FIVE-STAR Wealth Manager: http://www.fivestarprofessional.com
- Forbes, Steve: http://en.wikipedia.org/wiki/Steve_Forbes
- Forbes, Steve. Bio: http://www.forbes.com/fdc/bios/steveforbes.html
- Forbes, Steve. Forbes Online: http://www.forbes.com/
- Fundamental Analysis: http://en.wikipedia.org/wiki/Fundamental_analysis
- Future. Accessed May 2011: http://www.whitehouse.gov/CyberReview/

G.

- Generation X: http://en.wikipedia.org/wiki/Generation_X
- Generation Y: http://en.wikipedia.org/wiki/Generation_Y
- Google Container Data Center Tour: YouTube http://www.youtube.com/watch?v=zRwPSFpLX8I

H.

- Hathaway, Melissa. The White House Blog May 29, 2009 Securing Our Digital

- Home of the Future Control 4: http://control4.com/

- How Big Is the Internet?: http://netforbeginners.about.com/od/weirdwebculture/f/How-Big-Is-the-Internet.htm

I.

- Identity Theft Enforcement and Restitution Act 2008/The Computer Fraud and Abuse Act: http://en.wikipedia.org/wiki/Computer_Fraud_and_Abuse_Act http://www.justice.gov/criminal/cybercrime/ccmanual/01ccma.html

- IEEE Spectrum Magazine: http://spectrum.ieee.org/

- InfoWorld: http://www.infoworld.com/

- Investools: http://www.investools.com/

- Investors.com (eIBD): http://investors.com/

- iPod: http://en.wikipedia.org/wiki/IPod

- Investorideas.com - Cloud Stock News: Tickerspy.com Announces New Cloud Computing Stocks Index... April 11, 2011: http://www.investorideas.com/news/2011/main/04111.asp

- Irving Fisher: http://homepage.newschool.edu/het//profiles/fisher.htm

- iWatch, a Tiny, Wrist-Mounted iPhone, Gadget Lab by Charlie Sorrel May 10, 2010: http://www.wired.com/gadgetlab/2010/05/iwatch-a-tiny-wrist-mounted-iphone/

K.

- Kiwanis Family House: www.kiwanisfamilyhouse.org
- Komando. Kim Komando — The Kim Komando Show: www.komando.com

L.

- Lay, Todd: http://www.simplebackoffice.com/

M.

- MACD. Wikipedia on MACD: http://en.wikipedia.org/wiki/MACD
- Maslow, Abraham. 1943 Hierarchy of Needs: http://en.wikipedia.org/wiki/Maslow%27s_hierarchy_of_needs
- Meyer, Joseph. Bio: http://www.meyerassoc.com/experience.html
- Meyer, Joseph. Straight Money Analysis Website: http://straightmoneyanalysis.com/
- Mobile Magazine: http://www.mobilemag.com/
- Monster.com history: http://en.wikipedia.org/wiki/Monster.com
- Motley Fool. The Motley Fool website: www.fool.com

N.

- Nenner, Charles. Nenner Research Center: http://charlesnenner.com/

O.

- Online magazine – e-zine: http://en.wikipedia.org/wiki/Ezine
- Own the Clouds website: www.owntheclouds.com

- Ozzie, Ray. Memo: Dawn of a new day. MSFT: http://ozzie.net/docs/dawn-of-a-new-day/

P.

- PC Magazine: http://www.pcmag.com/
- PC World: http://www.pcworld.com/#new
- Pizza facts: http://thepizzajoint.com/pizzafacts.html

R.

- R&D: http://www.redherring.com/
- Rizzo, John. LinkedIn: http://www.linkedin.com/in/rizzojohn
- Roubini, Nouriel: http://pages.stern.nyu.edu/~nroubini/
- Roubini, Nouriel. Blog: http://www.roubini.com/

S.

- Satellite Direct Internet TV: http://www.digitalsatellite.tv/mac/win_user/download.html
- Sherlund, Rick. LinkedIn: http://www.linkedin.com/pub/rick-sherlund/5/121/750
- Sherlund, Rick. Twitter: http://twitter.com/#!/RickSher
- Sonders, Liz Ann: http://www.aboutschwab.com/press/experts/sonders.html
- Sonders, Liz Ann. Market Insight: http://www.schwab.com/public/schwab/research_strategies/market_insight?cmsid=P-980538&lvl1=research_strategies&lvl2=market_insight
- StockCharts.com: www.StockCharts.com
- Structural Change and Spatial Dynamics of the U.S. Software Industry Ted Egan, Ph.D. ICF Kaiser Intl Inc. April 25, 1998:

http://www.icfi.com/Publications/egan_sw.asp

- Summa, John, CTA, PhD, Founder of OptionsNerd.com and HedgeMyOptions.com. Forecasting Market Direction With Put/Call Ratios. June 17, 2010. Accessed September 2011. http://knowledgebase.mta.org/?fuseaction=kb. resource&kbDomainID=40723BA8-9D98-48B2-EE795C 07E1B4C2FE&kbResourceID=426427DA-E058-D2AC-C895A55033C77614

T.

- "The right to freedom of speech and expression." Wikipedia: http://en.wikipedia.org/wiki/Freedom_of_speech_and_ expression

- Tickerspy: http://tickerspy.com

U.

- U.S. Government Spending: http://it.usaspending. gov/?q=content/analysis http://www.nsf.gov/news/news_summ. jsp?cntn_id=117611

- US Patriot Act 2002: http://en.wikipedia.org/wiki/US_PATRIOT_ Act

W.

- Wadlin, Dr. Caroline Wadlin, M.D.: www.PreventBurnOutNow. com

- Web. Best of the Web Blogs (BOTW): http://blogs.botw.org/ Computers/

- Web browsers. Listed: http://en.wikipedia.org/wiki/List_of_web_ browsers

- Web search engine: http://en.wikipedia.org/wiki/Web_search_engine

- Wien, Byron: Predictions for 2011: http://reintell.com/byron-weins-predictions-for-2011/

- Wien, Byron: Prognosticator Byron Wien: The Outlook for '09, Take 2 by John Curran TIME, Mar 9, 2009: http://www.time.com/time/business/article/0,8599,1883828,00.html

- Wired: http://www.wired.com/

- World-newspapers.com: http://www.world-newspapers.com/computer.html

- World-newspapers.com. Technology Magazines Online: http://www.world-newspapers.com/technology.html

- Wozniak, Steve ("WOZ"): www.woz.org

Y.

- YouTube. Corning's "A Day Made of Glass." Video: http://www.youtube.com/watch?v=6Cf7IL_eZ38

- YouTube. Corning® Gorilla® Glass: TV. Commercial: http://www.youtube.com/watch?v=TVNkBG0SHws

- YouTube. Corning® Gorilla® Glass: "Cooking Up Tomorrow's Kitchen." Video: http://www.youtube.com/watch?v=ZUQEFL45Iko

- YouTube. "Google Data Center Tour." Video: http://www.youtube.com/watch?v=zRwPSFpLX8I

- YouTube. "The iWatch: Apple iPod nano 6G Wrist Watch Setup." Video: http://www.youtube.com/watch?v=C-K-piRoT8A

- YouTube. Monster 1999 Super Bowl Commercial: http://www.youtube.com/watch?v=rJB0CzlzSwY

INDEX

A.

Abuse. See Computer fraud, abuse; Cyber crime
Advertising, 27
Advice, financial, 130
    author special offer, 10, 154
    investment specialist, 135
Alerts, 136–138, 146
Analyst coverage (opinion), 73–76, 148
Analysts
    age factor, 92
    following, 103
    researching, choosing, 92–93
Annual blueprint, 151
Annual report, letter to shareholders, 151
Anti-malware, 41
Anti-spyware, 41
Applications (apps), 15, 18
Asia, Internet use, 34–35
ATMs, 16
Audit trail, 43
Autocorrelation, stock charts, 108–109, 113
Auto-erase, 43
Automobile industry, 2009 recession effect, 26
Avatars, personal, 23–24

B.

Backup, of data, 42
Balance sheet, 72, 80–81
Ballmer, Steve, 28

Banking. See Business, conducting online (business clouds)

Basic line chart, 114–117

Big cloud computing companies, 55, 64, 98

Big-dog companies, 70

Bill paying. See Business, conducting online (business clouds)

Bloggers, blogging, 93

Blonskij, Joyce

    advice, investment, special offer, 10

    biography, 153

    book, 154

    charitable giving, 159

    disclosure statements, 155–156

    following, 154

    hold harmless statement, 155–156

    special offer code, 154

    websites, 154

Blueprints

    annual, 151

    daily, 147–148

    first day, 146–147

    quarterly, 149–150

    weekly, 148

Bollinger Bands, 64, 121

    band squeeze, 122–123

    Cisco chart, 124–125

    components, 122

Bottom-up investing, 82–83

Brokerage account, 134

Broker/dealer disclosure statement, Joyce Blonskij, 155

Bumpy markets, 129–130

Business, conducting online (business clouds), 24–25

Business search engines, 89

Businesses, 2009 recession effect, 26

Buy-back, 101–102

C.

Calculators, early, 25

Cash flow, 72, 81–82

CBOE. See Chicago Board Options Exchange

Cell phones, 14

Chandrasekaran, N., 28

Change, embracing, 140

Change, technology driven, 4–5

Charging kit. See Solar panel charging kit

Charitable giving, Joyce Blonskij, 159

Charting services, 114, 149

Charting tools, 64

    basic line chart, 114–117

    Bollinger Bands, 64, 121–125

    Moving Average Convergence/Divergence, 119–121

    Stochastic Oscillator, Relative Strength Index, 125–126

Charts. See Stock charts

Chicago Board Options Exchange (CBOE), 114

Chief visionary officers (CVOs), 34

China, Internet use, 34–35

China, technology purchasing, 35–36

Chips. See Semiconductors sector

Cirrus clouds (high level), 64–65, 85–86. See also Bloggers, blogging;
    E-zines; Newsletters; Search engines

Cisco chart, 124–125

Cleaning, computer, 42

Cloud computing

    companies, 2

    defined, 6–7

    expansion, 28

Cloud computing stock index, 69

Cloud core list, 69

Cloud hosting, 50

Cloud index, 150

Clouds charity, Joyce Blonskij, 159

Cloud-ware. See Virtual (cloud-based) software

Communication technology

    evolution, development, 2, 4–5, 14–15

    as fad, 4–5

    as fashion, 22–23

Communications equipment sector, 56

Companies

    big cloud, 55, 64, 98

    big-dog, 70

    buy-back, 101–102

    choosing, questions, 9, 61

    competitors, 76–78, 99–100

    debt, 81

    field domination, 70

    financials, 72, 80–82

    growth, 81

    identification for investment, 64–65

    information, outside sources, 102

    Internet security, safety and, 37–41

    investor relations, 72, 98–99

    key statistics, 72, 79–80

    product, service advantage, 79–84

    profit growth, 79–84

    researching, 59–61, 68–69

    stock trend recognition, 65

Competitors

    comparison, 76–78

    quarterly blueprint, 150

    reverse engineering, 99–100

Computer cleaning, 42

Computer fraud, abuse, 38–39. See also Cyber crime

Computer industry sectors, 55–58

Computers, early, 14
Construction, 2009 recession effect, 26
Cost
    Internet service, 40–41
    savings, with virtual software, 46–47
    technology, declining, 25
Crime. See Cyber crime
Cumulus clouds (low level), 65, 107–108. See also Stock charts
CVOs. See Chief visionary officers
Cyber crime, 36–37. See also Computer fraud, abuse
Cyber policy, 39–40
Cycles, stock charts, 111–112

D.

Daily blueprint, 147–148
Data
    recovery plan, 43, 48–49
    safety, 42–43
    storage, archiving, 42–43, 48–51
Data centers (clouds), 48
    demand, future, 51
    energy usage increase, 51
    public, 49
    selecting, 49
    shift to, 48–49
Data components, stock charts, 110
Data points, stock charts, 109
"Day Made of Glass, A," 28
Day trading, long-term trend vs., 142
Debt, companies, 81
Dedicated hosting, 50
Dedicated servers, 50
Depression, Great, 26

Designers, developers. See Web designers, developers

Devices. See also specific devices

    ease of use, 41

    safety, 41–42

    storage, sector, 57

Digital video recorders (DVRs), 102

Disaster recovery plan, 43, 48–49

Disney, Walt, 11

Diversification, stock, 127, 129–130

DJIA. See Dow Jones Industrial Average

Dogs of the Dow, 70

DOS operating system, 47

DOS-based computers, 14

Dow Jones Industrial Average (DJIA), during Great Depression, 26

Dow Jones Industrial Stock Index, 70

Downgrades history, stock. See Upgrades, downgrades history, stock

DVRs. See Digital video recorders

E.

Earnings Before Interest, Taxes, Depreciation and
    Amortization (ttm), 77

Earnings Per Share (ttm), 77

Earnings release, quarterly, 149

EBITDA (ttm), 77

E-business, 2–3

Ecology, cloud computing and, 19

Economists, following, 103

Economy, U.S., history, 26

Edison, Thomas, 4

Education, 103

Electrical footprint, reduction incentives, 51

Electronic instruments, controls sector, 57–58

Electronic magazines, 94–96

Employees on payroll, 77

Encryption, 42, 57

Encyclopedia Britannica, 17

End of world, prediction, 26

Energy use increase, data centers, 51

Energy use, reduction incentives, 51

EPS (ttm). See Earnings Per Share (ttm)

Equipment, communications, sector, 56

Equipment, office, sector, 58

E-tailers, 60

Exhibit No. 1, Summary Page, Yahoo Finance, 72, 160

Experts, contacting, 104

E-zines, 94–96

F.

Facebook, 2, 17

Fashion statement, technology as, 22

File storage, 42–43, 48–51

Finance

    Yahoo Finance, 59, 69–70, 150

Finances, conducting online. See Business, conducting online

Financial advice, professional, 130

    author special offer, 10, 154

    investment specialist, 135

Financial bloggers, blogging, 93

Financial TV, 102

Financials, quarterly blueprint, 150

First day blueprint, 146–147

Fisher, Irving, 26

Five-Star Wealth ManagerSM – disclosure statement, 155

Footprint, electrical, reduction incentives, 51

Forbes, Steve, 103

Foreign investing, 36

Fraud. See Computer fraud, abuse; Cyber crime

Fundamental analysis (bottom-up investing), 82–83

Future forecasting, 113–114

Future, of clouds, 8

G.

GDP. See Gross domestic product, U.S.

Generation Z, 18

Google Alert, 92–93

Google Finance, 114, 117

Government, U.S., Internet security and, 38–40

Governments, cyberspace policy, 39–40

Governments, data storage, 50

GPS, 18

Great Depression, 26

"Green Clouds," 51

Gross domestic product (GDP), U.S., 27

Gross margin (ttm), 77

Growth, debt, companies, 81

Guidelines for investors, 152

H.

Hackers, hacking, 36–37, 42. See also Cyber crime

Hardware industry, sector, computer, 55–56

Headlines. See News, info, headlines

Hold harmless statement, Joyce Blonskij, 155

Hologram TV, 23

Homes, smart, 25

Hosting, private cloud options, 50

Housing, 2009 recession effect, 26

Hybrid hosting, 50

I.

IAB. See Interactive Advertising Bureau

Identity protection. See Cyber crime

Income statement, companies, 79–80

Index, cloud, 150

India, 34–35

Industry

    2009 recession effect on, 26

    defined, 55

    sectors, computer, 55–58

    subgroups, technology, 59–60

Information sources, outside, 102

Insider transactions, 72, 100–102, 148

Instruments, controls, electronic, sector, 57–58

Instruments, scientific, technical, sector, 58

Insurance, devices, 42

Intelligent Information Laboratory (InfoLab), 23

Interactive Advertising Bureau (IAB), 27

Internet advertising, 27

Internet retail companies, 60

Internet search engines. See Search engines

Internet service cost, 40–41

Internet Services Disruption memo, The, 55

Internet use

    American, 4

    Asia, 34–35

    measurement, 4

Investment

    advice, professional, 10, 135, 154

    decisions, 142–144

    tips, 140–143

Investor relations, 98–99

Investors, guidelines, 152

J.

Japan tsunami, earthquake, 5
Jobs, 2009 recession effect, 26–27
Jobs, cloud-related, 27–28
Jobs, Steve, 17, 22
Journalists, following, 103
Junk mail. See Spam

K.

Kaku, Michio, 28
Key cloud (investing) elements, 9–10, 64–65
Key statistics, companies, 72, 79–80
Keywords, alerts, 136
Kiwanis Family House, 159

L.

Last trade, 71–73
Licensing agreements, 98–99
Lifestyle change, technology driven, 4–5
Long-term trend vs. day trading, 142

M.

MACD. See Moving Average Convergence/Divergence
Magazines, 94
Malware. See Anti-malware
Management effectiveness, 79–80
Managing stocks. See Process
Market cap (capitalization), 77
Market industry, sector, 55
Market sentiment, 114

Markets, bumpy, stocks, 129–130

Markets, cloud, 28

Medications, cloud computing and, 19

Meyer, Joseph, 103

Microprocessor chips, 58

Microsoft, 28, 54–55

Military, U.S., Internet security and, 38

Monitoring stocks online, 134–135

Monster.com, 46

Moving Average Convergence/Divergence (MACD), 119–121

N.

Nenner, Charles, 103

Net income (ttm), 77

Networking sector, computer, 56–57

News, info, headlines, 72, 82, 148

News search engines, 89–90

Newsletters, 93–94

Newspapers, circulation decline, 5

O.

Obama, Barack, 38–39

Offer, exclusive, from author, 10, 154

Office equipment sector, 58

One-year target estimate, 71–73

Operating margin (ttm), 77

Option disclosure statement, Joyce Blonskij, 155–156

Options exchange, 114

Outside sources, information, 102, 148

Ownership, insider transactions, 100–102

Ozzie, Ray, 54

P.

Paper trades, 136

Passwords, 41–43, 57

Past trailing twelve months (ttm), 77–78

P/E (ttm). See Price to Earnings Ratio (ttm)

PEG (5 yr expected). See Price Earnings Growth (5 year expected)

Pension plans, public, 104

Peripherals sector, computer, 57

Polar clouds (highest level), 64, 67–69. See also Big cloud computing companies

Policy. See Cyber policy

Pony Express, 2

Portfolio check, 134–135

Postal Service, U.S., 27

Price Earnings Growth (5 year expected), 78

Price Earnings (P/E) Ratio, 71

Price target summary, stock, 73–74

Price to Earnings Ratio (ttm), 77

Price-to-sales ratio (ttm), 78

Privacy laws, vendors and, 43

Private data centers (private clouds), 49–50

Process, 133–143. See also Blueprints

    alerts, 136–138

    brokerage account, 134

    change, embracing, 140

    investment decisions, 142–143

    investment tips, 140–143

    long-term trend vs. day trading, 142

    paper trades, 136

    portfolio check, 134–135

    reference guides, complimentary, 138–139

    stock summary, 147

    system, low- vs. high-tech, 146

trends, following, 140–141
Product, service advantage, 79–84
Profile (investor relations), companies, 72, 98–99
Profit growth, 79–84
Programming sector, 58
P/S (ttm). See Price-to-sales ratio (ttm)
Public data centers (public clouds), 49
Public pension plans, 104
Purchasing, payments, 18–19
Put/call ratios, 113–114

Q.

Quarterly blueprint, 149–150
Quarterly Revenue Growth (year over year), 77
Questions, choosing companies, 9, 61

R.

Rabini, Nouriel, 103
Radio-Frequency IDentification (RFID), 36
Rating categories, stocks, 74–75
Really Simple Syndication feed. See RSS feed
Recession, 2009, U.S., 26–27
Recommendation summary, stock, 73
Recommendation trends, stock, 75–76
Recovery plan, data, 43, 48–49
Reference guides, complimentary, 138–139
Reports, analyst, 76
Research
    companies, 68–69
    stocks, pre-Internet, 68
Researching companies, 59–61. See also Reverse engineering; Search
        engines; Yahoo Finance

Revenue (ttm), 77
Reverse engineering, 98–99
RFID. See Radio-Frequency IDentification
RSI. See Stochastic Oscillator, Relative Strength Index
RSS feed, 92, 146, 148

S.

S & P. See Standard & Poor's
Safety, security. See also Computer fraud, abuse; Cyber crime
    companies, 37–41
    data, 42–43
    devices, 41–42
Salaries, cloud-related, 27–28
Scientific, technical instruments sector, 58
Search engines, 86, 88–90
Searches, specific, 90–92
Seasonality, stock charts, 112
SEC. See U.S. Securities and Exchange Commission
Sectors, technology industry, 55–60
Security. See Computer fraud, abuse; Cyber crime; Safety, security
Semiconductors sector, 58
Servers. See also Data centers (clouds)
    dedicated, 50
    demand for, 51
    renting, 50
    virtual vs. in-house, 46
Service advantage, companies, 79–84
Services sector, computer, 57
Shareholders, annual report, letter, 151
Sherlund, Rick, 103
Smart homes, 25
Smartphones, 14
Smartphone/wristwatch, 22

Social media, 17–18. See also Facebook; Twitter

Software

    industry, 55

    programming sector, 58

    structural shift, 54

    upgrading, 47

    virtual (cloud-based), 46–47

Solar panel charging kit, 42

Sonders, Liz Ann, 103

Spam, 46–47

Special offer, author financial advice, 10, 154

Spyware. See Anti-spyware

Standard & Poor's (S & P), 68, 76

Starbucks, 15

Statements, financial, investment. See Business, conducting online (business clouds)

Statistics, key, companies, 72, 79–80

Staying current. See Process

Stochastic Oscillator, Relative Strength Index (RSI), 125–126

Stock charts, 126–127. See also Charting tools

    autocorrelation, 108–109, 113

    basic tech analysis, 72, 126

    blueprint, weekly, 149

    charting services, 114

    cycles, 111–112

    data components, 110

    data points, 109

    key cloud element, 64–65, 107–108

    options exchange, 114

    put/call ratios, 113–114

    seasonality, 112

    surprises, 112

    time series analysis, 109–110

    trends, 110–111, 113, 118

Stock index, 69
Stock market, Great Depression and, 26
Stock reports, 68, 76
Stock summary, 147
Stock Watch Alert, 137
StockCharts.com, 114
Stocks
    bumpy markets, 129–130
    price, as factor, 70
    price change, response, 127–128
    rating categories, 74–75
    researching, pre-Internet, 68
    selling, 128–129
    trend recognition, 65
    upgrades, downgrades, 74–76
Storage, data, files, 42–43, 48–51
Storage devices sector, computer, 57
Stratus clouds (mid level), 65, 97–98. See also Reverse engineering
Structural change, 15–19, 54
Summary Page, Yahoo Finance, 71–73, 160
Surprises, stock charts, 112
System, low- vs. high-tech, 146

T.

Taylor, Jeff, 46
Tech bloggers, blogging, 93
Tech Sector Directory, 69
Technical instruments sector, 58
Technology. See also Communication technology
    costs, declining, 25
    security, safety, 39–40
Technology, cloud-based, future, 17–19
Technology sector

choosing companies, questions, 9, 61

groups, 55–60

industry subgroups list, 59–60

Telecommunications industry, 55

Telecommuting, 35

3-D TV, 23

Time series analysis, 109–110

Trade shows, 87–88

Trends

following, 140–141

long-term vs. day trading, 142

recommendation, stock, 75–76

Trends, stock charts, 110–111

spotting, recognition, 65, 118

strong vs. weak, 113

Ttm. See Past trailing twelve months

TV, financial, 102

Twitter, 5, 147–148

U.

Upgrades, downgrades history, stock, 74–75

U.S. government, military, Internet security and, 38–40

U.S. Postal Service, Internet effect on, 27

U.S. Securities and Exchange Commission (SEC), 100

V.

VCS. See Video communication system

Vendors, safety and, 42–43

Video communication system (VCS), 25

· Video recorders, digital (DVRs), 102

Videos. See YouTube

Virtual server, 46–47

Virtual (cloud-based) software, 46–47
Visionaries, 34
Volatility, stocks, 124–125

W.

Wall Street news, info, 148
Wall Street stock rating, 73–75
Walmart, 70
Walton, Sam, 70
Watson, Thomas, 4
Web applications (cloud-ware), 46–47
Web browsers, 86
Web designers, developers, 27–28
Web link disclosure statement, Joyce Blonskij, 156
Weekly blueprint, 148–149
Wien, Byron, 103
Windows operating system, 46
Wireless devices, 19
Wozniak, Steve, 22
Wristwatch/smartphone, 22

Y.

Yahoo alerts, 136–137
Yahoo Finance, 59, 69–70, 150
    analyst coverage (opinion), 73–76
    annual reports, 98–99
    balance sheet, 72, 80
    cash flow, 72, 81–82
    charts, basic tech analysis, 126
    competitors, 76–78, 99–100
    insider transactions, 72, 100–102
    investor relations, 72, 98–99

key statistics, 72, 79–80
last trade, 71–73
licensing agreements, 98–99
news, info, headlines, 72, 82, 148
one-year target estimate, 71–73
price target summary, 73–74
recommendation summary, 73
recommendation trends, 75–76
reviews, quarterly, 126
Summary Page, 71–73, 160
upgrades, downgrades history, 74–75
Yahoo technology sector, 59–60
YouTube, 86–87

CPSIA information can be obtained at www.ICGtesting.com
Printed in the USA
BVOW011217290212

284086BV00006B/385/P